Friendship an

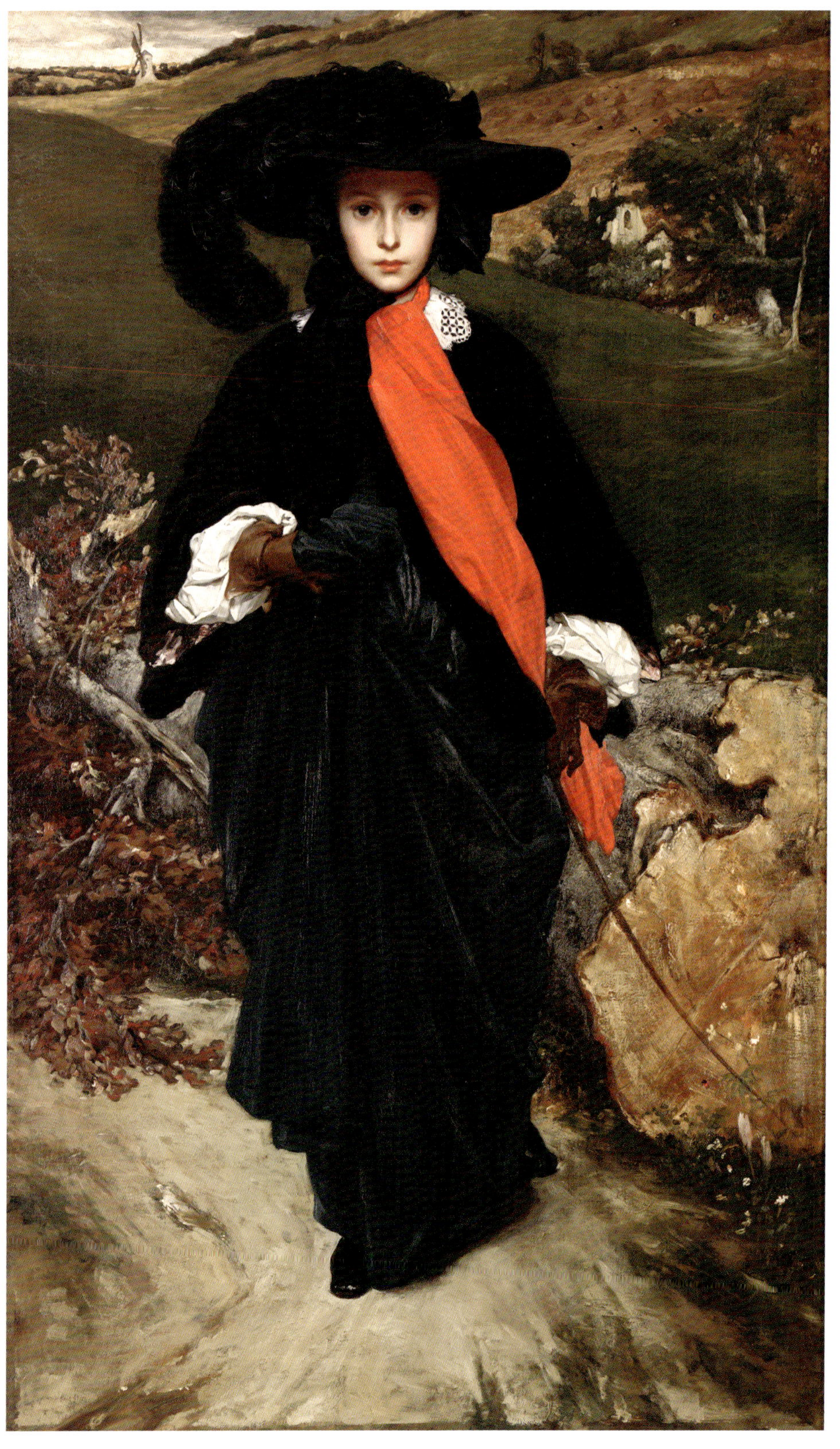

KIMBELL MASTERPIECE SERIES

Friendship and Loss in the Victorian Portrait

May Sartoris BY FREDERIC LEIGHTON

MALCOLM WARNER

Kimbell Art Museum
Fort Worth

DISTRIBUTED BY
Yale University Press
New Haven and London

KIMBELL MASTERPIECE SERIES

Published by the Kimbell Art Museum, Fort Worth
Distributed by Yale University Press, New Haven and London

Kimbell Art Museum
3333 Camp Bowie Boulevard
Fort Worth, Texas 76107-2792
www.kimbellart.org

Yale University Press
302 Temple Street
P.O. Box 209040
New Haven, Connecticut 06520-9040
www.yalebooks.com

Produced by the Publications Department of the Kimbell Art Museum
Wendy P. Gottlieb, Manager of Publications
Megan Burns, Editorial and Publications Assistant
With thanks to Robert LaPrelle, Judy Mahan, and Mark Marr

Designed by Tom Dawson

Printed in Singapore by CS Graphics

Library of Congress Control Number: 2009925866

ISBN: 978-0-300-12135-3

COVER, INSIDE FLAP, AND FRONTISPIECE: Frederic Leighton, *May Sartoris*, c. 1860. Oil on canvas, 59⅞ x 35½ in. (152.1 x 90.2 cm). Kimbell Art Museum, Fort Worth

Contents

FAMILY TREE

KEMBLE
DE CAMP
Sarah (Mrs. Siddons)
1755–1831
John Philip
1757–1823
Frances (Fanny)
1759–1822
Charles
1775–1854
m.
1806
Marie-Thérèse
1774–1838
John Mitchell
1807–1857
m.
1836
Natalie Augusta Wendt
Frances Anne (Fanny)
1809–1893
m.
1834
Pierce Butler
1806–1867
divorced 1849
Henry James Vincent
1812–1857

Catherine Hermione
1872–1956
Jean Adelaide
1873–1954
m.
1899
Lt.-Gen. Sir William
Thomas Furse
1865–1953
David Gordon Roberts
1900–1955
Diana
1902–1931
Roger Kemble
1903–1972
Judith
1912–1974

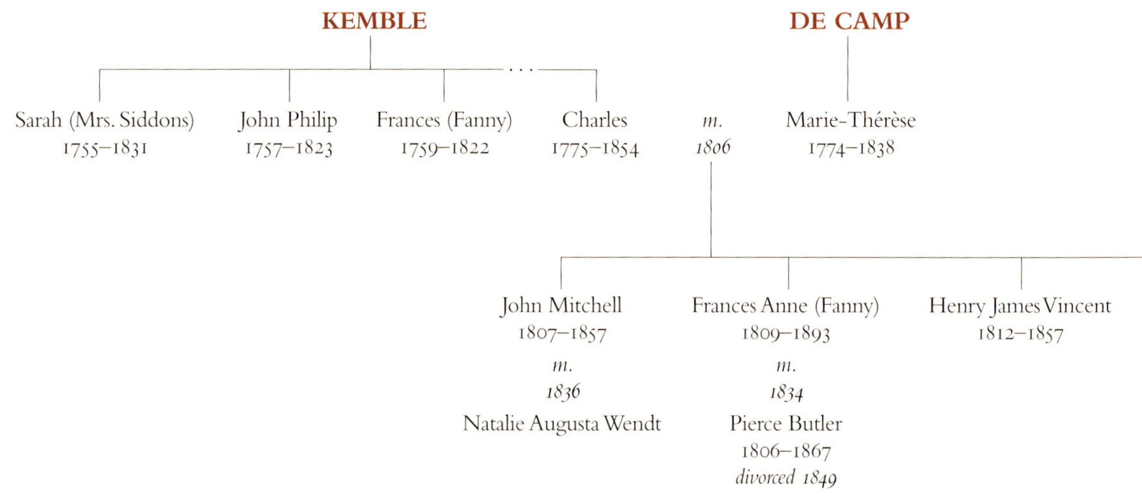

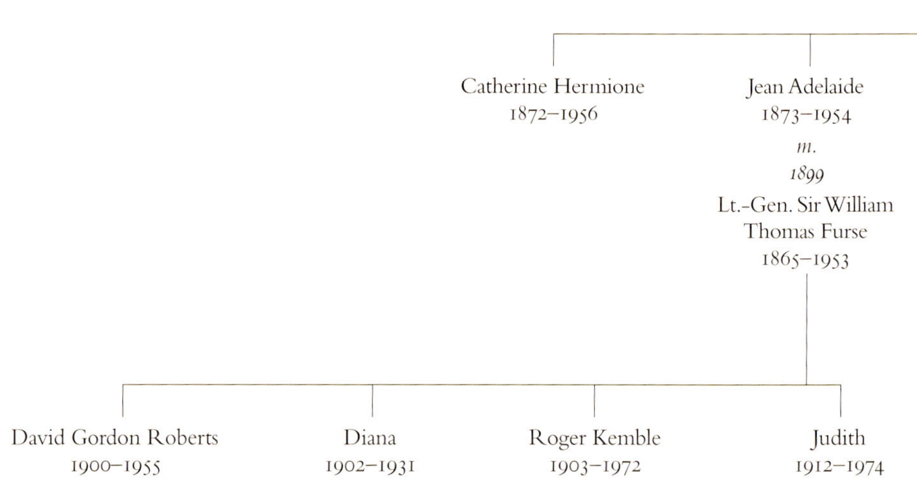

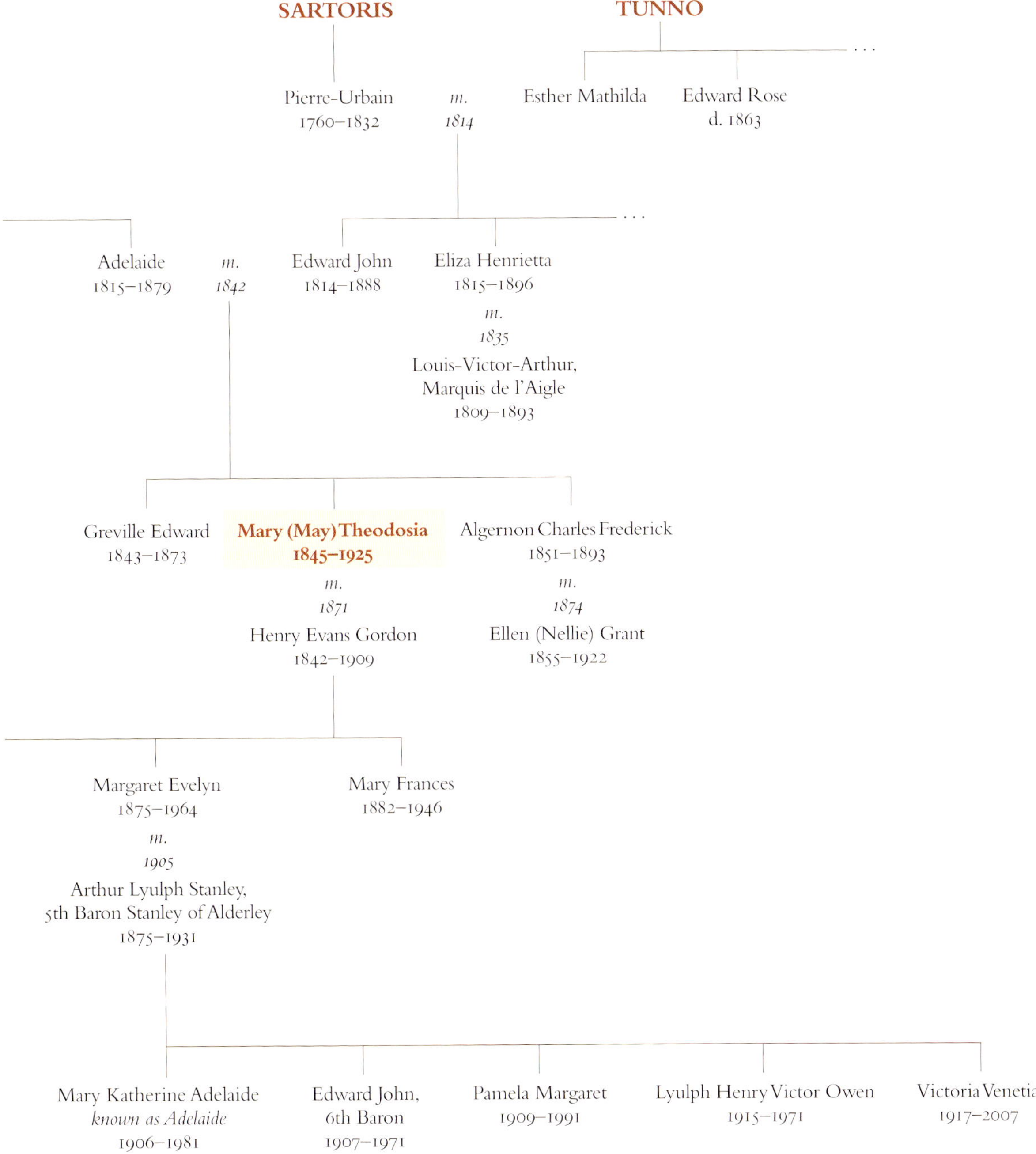
SARTORIS
TUNNO
Pierre-Urbain
1760–1832
m.
1814
Esther Mathilda
Edward Rose
d. 1863
Adelaide
1815–1879
m.
1842
Edward John
1814–1888
Eliza Henrietta
1815–1896
m.
1835
Louis-Victor-Arthur,
Marquis de l'Aigle
1809–1893
Greville Edward
1843–1873
Mary (May) Theodosia
1845–1925
m.
1871
Henry Evans Gordon
1842–1909
Algernon Charles Frederick
1851–1893
m.
1874
Ellen (Nellie) Grant
1855–1922
Margaret Evelyn
1875–1964
m.
1905
Arthur Lyulph Stanley,
5th Baron Stanley of Alderley
1875–1931
Mary Frances
1882–1946
Mary Katherine Adelaide
known as Adelaide
1906–1981
Edward John,
6th Baron
1907–1971
Pamela Margaret
1909–1991
Lyulph Henry Victor Owen
1915–1971
Victoria Venetia
1917–2007

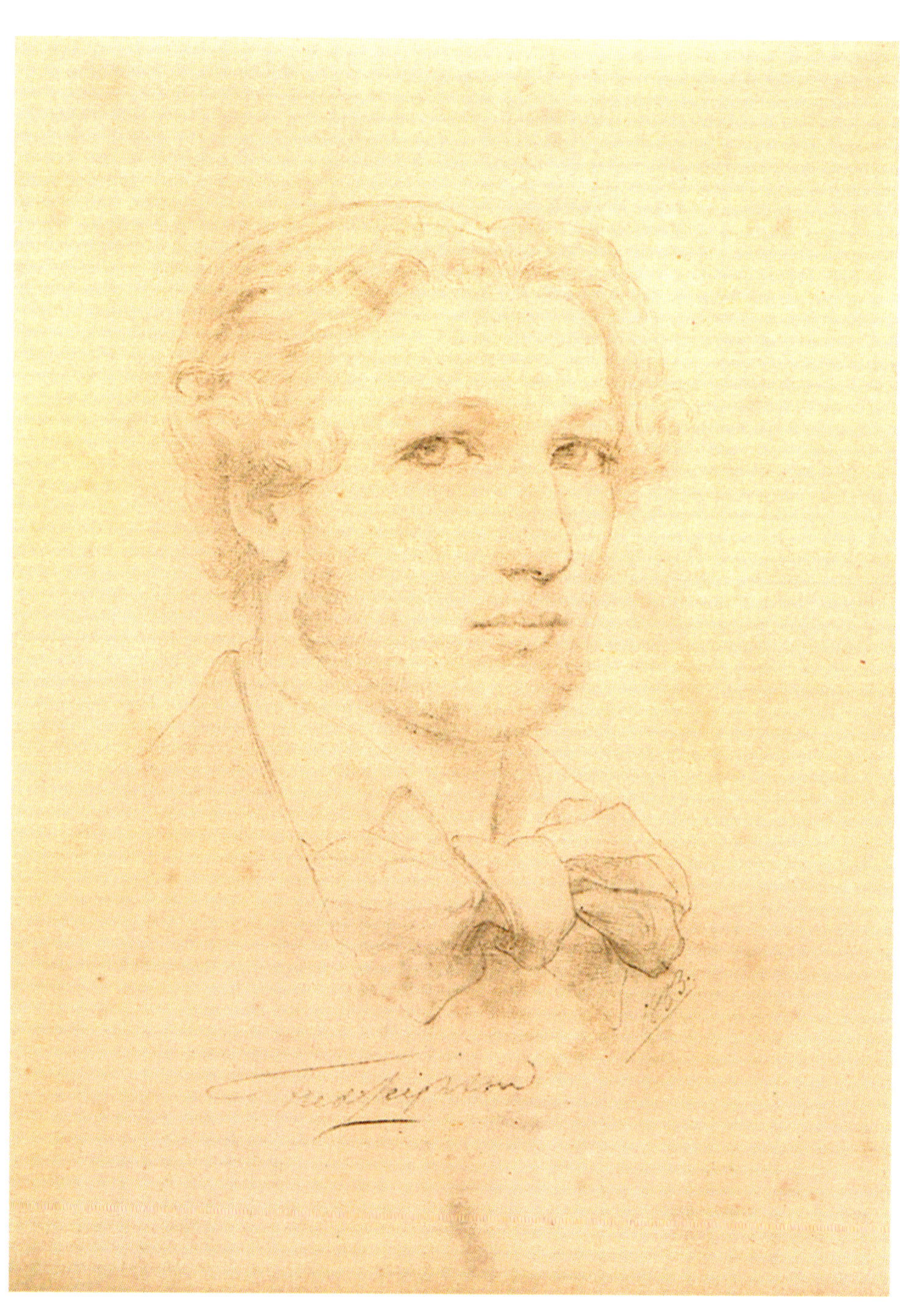

Adelaide and Fay

IN EARLY FEBRUARY 1853 A YOUNG ARTIST AND A RETIRED OPERA SINGER MET IN ROME and began a lifelong friendship. Frederic Leighton was twenty-two years old, handsome, charming, and clearly, to all who knew him, a man with a bright future. He was immaculately well mannered and showed a flair for foreign languages, which he spoke fluently and with a perfect accent. Since he was nine, he and his parents had led a largely expatriate life. His father was a doctor of independent means, and, for the benefit of his mother's uncertain health, the family made long tours on the Continent and lived for periods in Italy, Germany, Belgium, and France. "Although he had the unmistakable look of an Englishman," a friend recalled, "there was a foreign tone about him, mingled with the *bel air* of the best cosmopolitan society."[1] At fifteen he had enrolled as an art student at the Städelsches Kunstinstitut in Frankfurt. There he studied with Edward von Steinle, one of the German Renaissance revivalists known as the Nazarenes. He painted scenes from the lives of artistic heroes of the Renaissance, and his most ambitious work to date was *The Death of Brunelleschi*.[2] He arrived in Rome late in 1852 armed with introductions to the Nazarene painters Peter Cornelius and Johann Friedrich Overbeck. His principal work of the next two years was the first in a series of large, friezelike compositions with many figures that would punctuate his career, *Cimabue's Celebrated Madonna Is Carried in Procession through the Streets of Florence*.[3]

Opposite page: Frederic Leighton, *Self-Portrait*, 1853. Pencil, 9¼ x 7 in. (23.5 x 18 cm). Private collection

Adelaide Sartoris, about to be thirty-eight years old and already ten years into her retirement from the stage, was acclaimed as one of the finest singers England had ever produced. She came from the illustrious English theatrical family of the Kembles. Her father, the actor and theater manager Charles Kemble, was the younger brother of John Philip Kemble and Sarah Siddons, both giants of the English theater, and in her own generation the torch of drama had passed to her older sister, Fanny Kemble. Adelaide trained at the Paris Conservatoire and made her professional debut at La Fenice, Venice, in 1838, singing the title role in Bellini's *Norma*. She went on to glory across Italy and then two brilliant seasons at Covent Garden in London. She made the challenging role of Norma her own and, not surprisingly given her lineage, was lauded as a singer who could also act (fig. 1). If she had a fault, it was a tendency to put acting before singing. "She was apt," wrote her admirer Anna Jameson, "to sacrifice the music, the vocal intonation, to the more emphatic expression of character or passion."[4] Her career was short. In 1842 she married the wealthy Edward Sartoris and left professional singing behind as an occupation not befitting a respectable wedded woman. Jameson recalled her emotional final exit at Covent Garden: "On recovering herself, in her dressing-room, she looked at the laurel-wreath and flowers, still clasped in her hand, and exclaimed, with a gush of mournful feeling: 'What!—is it all over?—And is this *all* that remains?'"[5]

Since that time she had devoted her time to running a household, raising children, and social life, both in the high circles into which Edward introduced her and in the musical, literary, and artistic ones that she preferred. She still sang—for select audiences, never for money—and, as the novelist William Makepeace Thackeray noted after hearing her at a soirée in London, her voice was still strong: "She was passionate, she was enthusiastic, she was sublime, she was tender—there was one note wh. she kept so long, that I protest I had time to think about my affairs, to have a little nap, and to wake much refreshed, whilst it was going on still—at another time overcome by almost unutterable tenderness she piped so low that it's a wonder one could hear at all—in a word she was *mirobolante*, the most artless affected good-natured absurd clever creature possible."[6]

Though brought up English, Adelaide's husband Edward Sartoris was from a Continental background, and in her eyes this was no doubt part of his attraction. His father was a Piedmontese banker, his mother was Anglo-Italian, and there was money on both sides

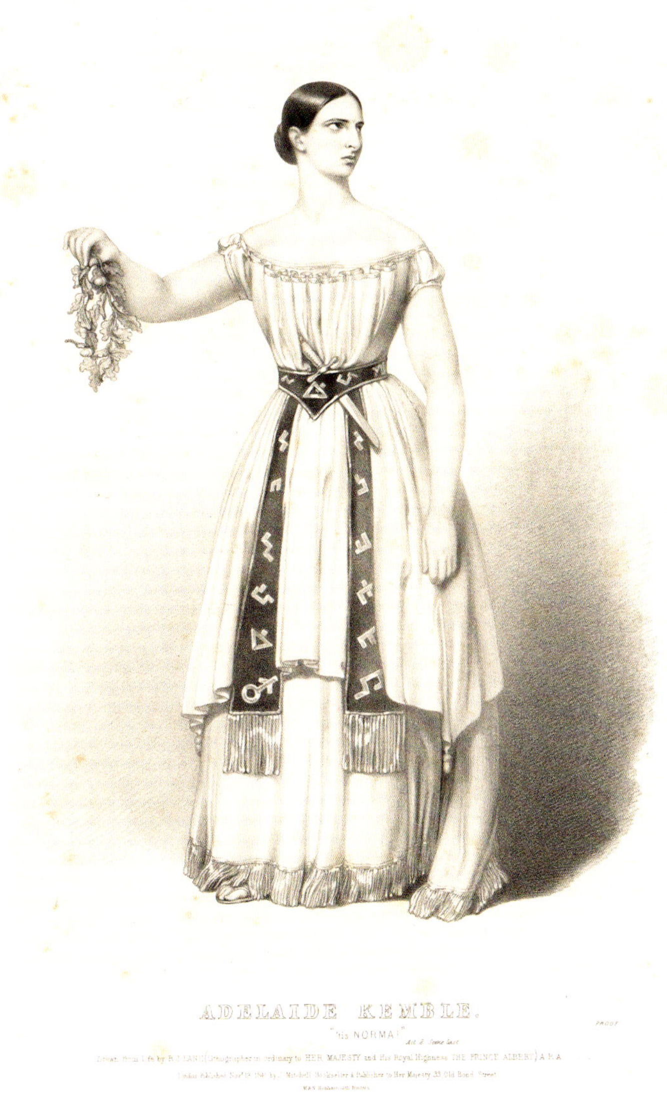

Fig. 1. *Adelaide Kemble as Norma*, 1841. Lithograph by Richard James Lane, publ. John Mitchell, sheet: 21⅜ x 14½ in. (54.2 x 36.8 cm). National Portrait Gallery, London

of the family. His sister Eliza married a French aristocrat, the marquis de l'Aigle. Edward was a gentleman of considerable independent means who pursued no profession. He was interested in politics and the arts, had a pleasant voice, took singing lessons, and enjoyed amateur theatricals. According to Leighton's biographer Mrs. Russell Barrington, he was "a fairly good amateur artist, and was considered by his friends to be a first-rate critic of painting."[7] Adelaide was fond of him: "His voice is gentle and his manner of speaking and manner in general are slow and indolent—he is tolerant and generous and tender hearted in the extreme—he is of a most grateful and affectionate nature—and utterly incapable of malicious or rancorous feeling—I think he is the most humble and modest person I ever knew—his temper is very even and he is *perfectly* easy to live with—to love—to trust and to be happy with."[8] Compared to the brilliant musical, artistic, and literary figures with whom Adelaide surrounded herself, however, he was dull. Her old friend Theodosia Monson heard the news of her engagement from Anna Jameson and wrote back in astonishment: "*Not* handsome, *not* ugly, *not* fat, *not* thin, *not* good, *not* bad, *not* pleasant, *not* unpleasant, in short the only quality about him not negative [is] that he always has his hands in his P. Jacket. I cannot make it out; when I talked to A. about marrying a good man she could esteem and not to marry from any superabundance of the *belle passion*, I did *not* think of Sartoris; I did not mean her to go as far as that . . . I don't see that she will be *un*happy, I don't see that she will be happy. I shall not be *surprised* if you tell me *he* dances on the *tight rope*, but if you tell me A. is in love with him, I shall."[9] Henry James, another Adelaide devotee, would describe Edward as "her taciturn husband (the perfect ideal of the ill-mannered Englishman who improves—somewhat—on acquaintance)."[10]

Adelaide had attracted many male admirers, notably Lord John Cavendish Bentinck-Scott, Marquess of Titchfield (later 5th Duke of Portland), who courted her ardently and commissioned Francis Grant to paint a portrait of her in the title role of Rossini's *Semiramide* (fig. 2).[11] But the love of her life was a central European nobleman rather than a British one. She met Francis Thun, the son and heir of Count Franz Anton von Thun-Hohenstein of Tetschen Castle in northern Bohemia, while traveling with her father for his health. She and Thun fell in love, but he stopped short of proposing marriage. Perhaps too quickly, Adelaide gave up hope of his ever doing so and closed the door on the possibility by going professional as a singer. Now she led a comfortable life with the steady Edward, and enjoyed her friends and children. But she had sacrificed both love and career—the first by taking to the stage, the second by leaving it—and the emotional cost was great. She would occasionally confide in friends a sense of regret and disappointment: "I should be happy but I *cannot*."[12] Her features were still striking but since her retirement she had lost the trim figure of her

Fig. 2. Francis Grant, *Adelaide Kemble as Semiramide*, 1842. Oil on canvas, 94 x 58½ in. (238.8 x 148.6 cm). Private collection

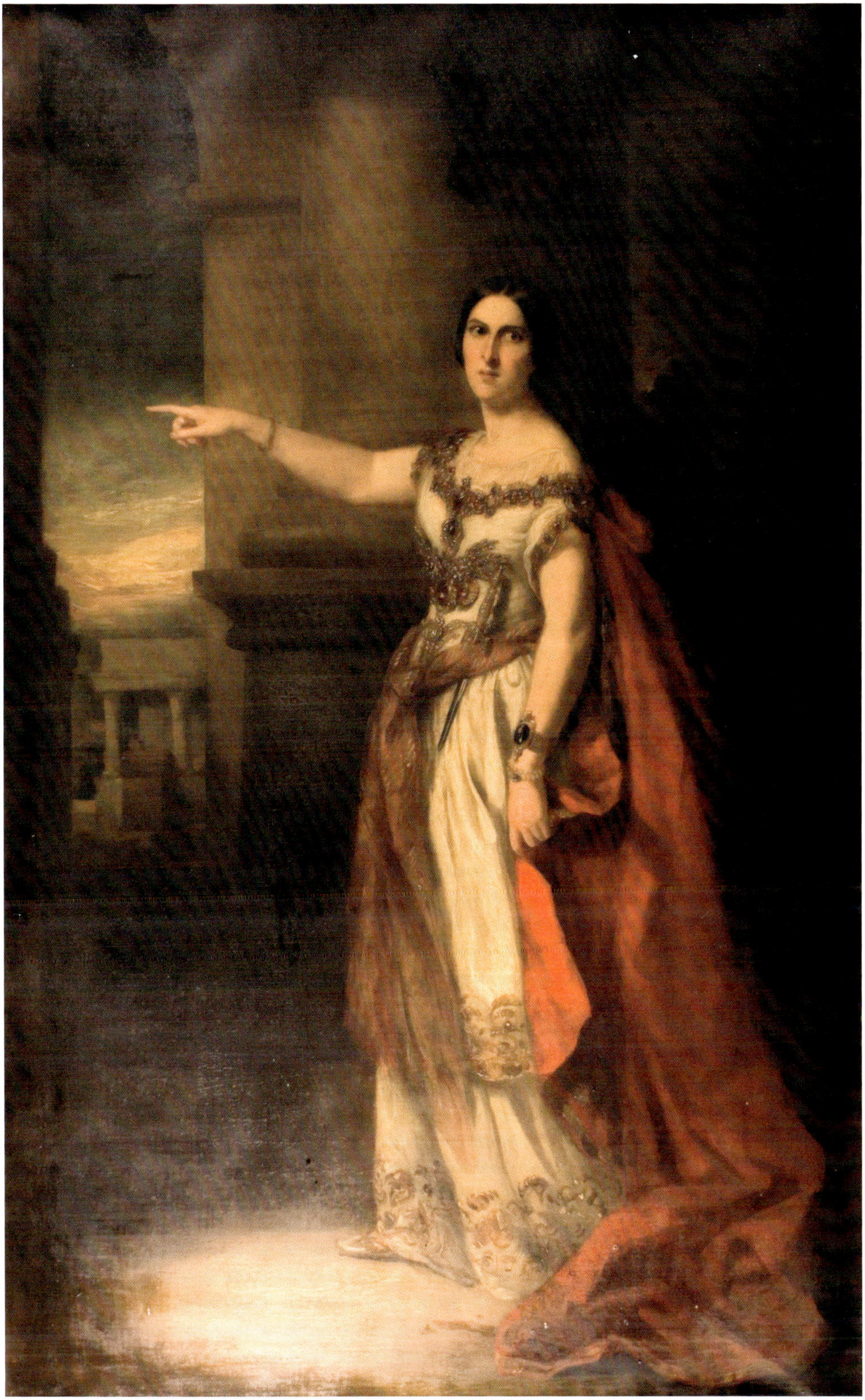

5

youth to obesity. "Only her head has remained like a cameo," observed her friend Frédéric Chopin.[13]

The Sartorises lived between England, France, and Italy, leasing various houses and apartments and traveling frequently. Adelaide had been passionate about Italy since her singing debut, and during her Covent Garden years set her heart on retiring there. Knowing Italian as the language of most of her operatic roles, and never immune to affectation, she readily dropped Italian phrases into her conversation and writing. Early in their marriage, between 1845 and 1848, she and Edward had already lived in Italy for a period.[14] When she met Leighton in 1853, they had come for another extended stay, during which they leased an apartment in Rome for the winter months and spent the summers traveling and visiting resorts such as Bagni di Lucca, Sorrento, and Amalfi. While in Rome Adelaide was hostess to an artistic salon frequented by the poets Robert and Elizabeth Barrett Browning. Her circle also included Thackeray, who was an old friend of her brother John; the American sculptress Harriet Hosmer; Charles Hamilton Aïdé, an aspiring artist and writer; Richard Lyons, a cheery British diplomat; and the distinguished French historian Jean-Jacques Ampère. Now divorced from the American plantation-owning husband for whom she had left the stage, her sister Fanny Kemble came to stay for a time and added further luster to the company.

Adelaide took a great liking to Leighton, and soon he became a regular at her Sunday and Wednesday soirées. She would sing for the company and have others join her, encouraging Leighton to show off a good tenor voice. Fanny would perform the one-woman readings from Shakespeare with which she so successfully toured Britain and the United States at this period of her career. There were *tableaux vivants* and charades. As Fanny later recalled, the group would get together for picnics in the countryside: "We had an excellent custom of going on alternate weeks to spend a morning in the Campagna, always accompanied by the same party of our intimate friends, and carrying with us our picnic lunch. We used to leave our carriages, and stray and wander and sit on the turf, and take our luncheon in the midst of all that was lovely in nature and picturesque in the ruined remains of Roman power and the immortal memories of Roman story. They were hours in such fellowship never to be forgotten."[15] This charmed society embraced Leighton as a young man full of talent and promise. On returning to London, Thackeray told the already celebrated young painter

John Everett Millais: "Millais, my boy, you must look to your laurels. There's a young fellow in Rome called Leighton who is making prodigious strides in his art. He speaks every European language, and is an accomplished musician as well. If I'm not mistaken that young man will one day be President of the Royal Academy."[16]

Leighton and Adelaide formed a bond as fellow expatriates and people of the world. Both had trained abroad for their professions, traveled widely on the Continent, and gained an impressive command of languages. As Leighton's devotion to Adelaide grew, so did a certain self-satisfaction and snobbery on his part at being part of such a glamorous circle. He wrote to his family:

> The more I enjoy and appreciate the society and intercourse of the dozen people that I care to know, the more tiresome I find the commerce of the others, *braves et excellentes gens du reste*; the Lord be merciful to the overwhelming insipidity of that individual whose name is Legion—the *unexceptionable*—the *highly respectable*! My great resource is, of course, Mrs. Sartoris, whom I see at some time or other every day, for it would be a blank day to me in which I did not see her; God bless her! for my dearest friend. I warm my very soul in the glow of her sisterly affection and kindness.[17]

Leighton and Adelaide had enough in common to make the age difference between them no barrier to intimate friendship. The fondness comes through in his tender drawings of her, caught as though looking down at one of her children or listening intently to a friend (figs. 3, 4). At times Adelaide seemed like an older sister to him, at times like a mother. On September 20, 1854, he wrote to his actual mother in England:

> As for that apprehension of yours, dearest Mamma, about my being alone and uncared for in case of illness, I am happy to say that nothing can be more unfounded; I have in Mrs. Sartoris that genuine friend, and, especially, genuine *woman friend* that in such a case would leave nothing undone that you, the best of mothers, and my own dear sisters, would do for me. It is her habit, when any of her bachelor and homeless friends are poorly, to go and sit with them and nurse them, and do you

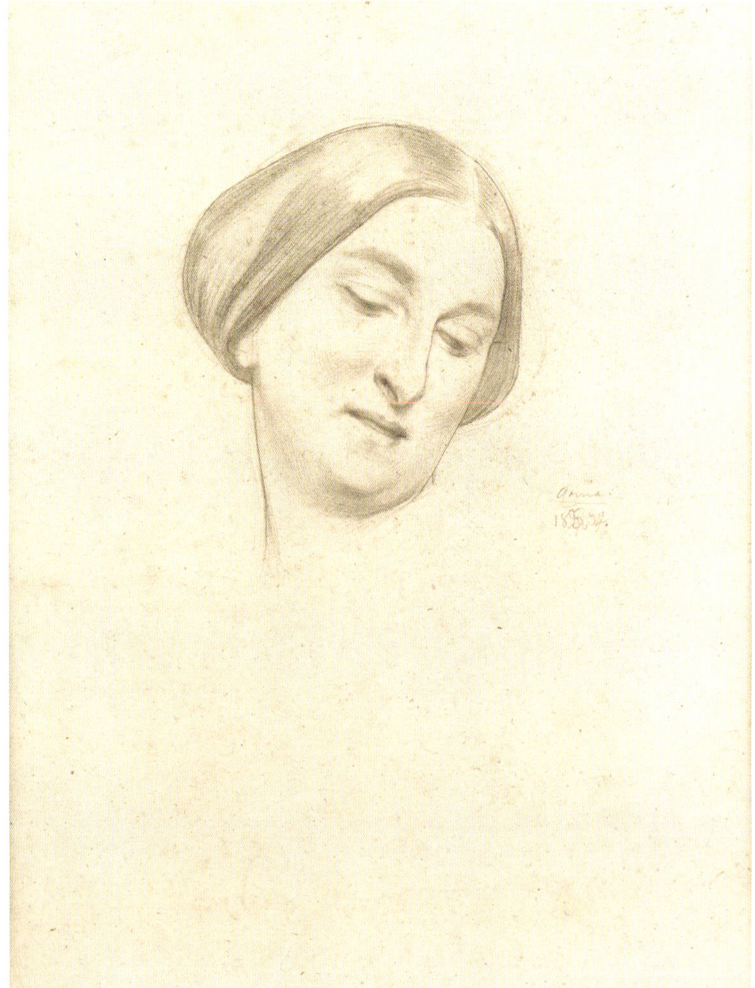

Fig. 3. Frederic Leighton, *Adelaide Sartoris*, 1854. Pencil, 11 x 8 in. (27.9 x 20.3 cm). Private collection

think that I, who have become one of her most intimate circle, should need to fear neglect? In the friendship of that admirable woman I am rich for life.[18]

She was delighted at his love of music, he at her love of art. Years later a friend of Adelaide's would contrast her with her sister Fanny: "Mrs. Kemble, so essentially poetic and dramatic in her nature; Mrs. Sartoris, so much of an artist, musical, with a love for exquisite things, and all that belongs to form and colour. (Some of us can remember hearing Lord Leighton say that though Mrs. Sartoris did not paint, she was a true painter in her sense of beauty of composition, in her great feeling for art.)"[19] At a time when British taste in art

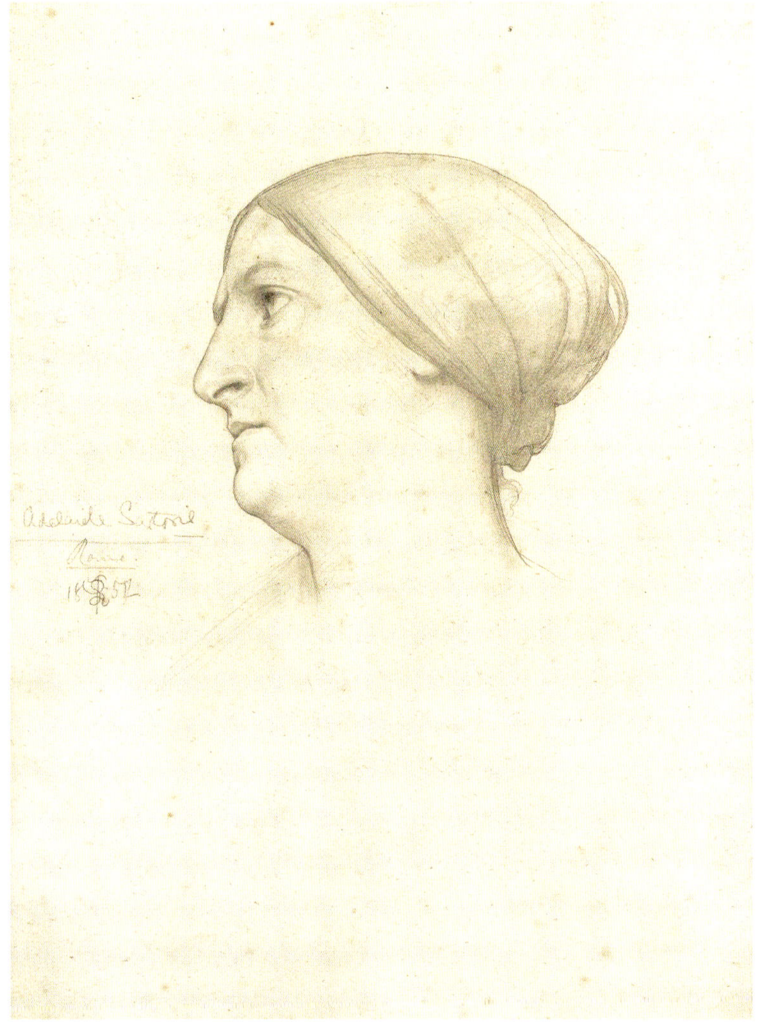

Fig. 4. Frederic Leighton, *Adelaide Sartoris*, 1854. Pencil, 11 x 8 in. (27.9 x 20.3 cm). Private collection

tended toward the factual, the narrative, and the moral, Adelaide and Leighton prized above all else the beautiful. Their shared devotion to "exquisite things and all that belongs to form and colour" would flow naturally into that tendency in progressive British art, architecture, and design known as the Aesthetic Movement. For them, as for all those of the aesthetic persuasion, it would be a quasi-religious life principle. "Now to love anything sincerely is an act of grace," Adelaide once wrote, "but to love the best sincerely is a state of grace."[20]

Another member of Adelaide's Roman circle, Viscount Fordwich, remarked that Leighton was "inseparable from Mrs. Sartoris (without scandal)."[21] They were so close that people thought about the possibility that they might be having an affair; otherwise Fordwich's statement would have been redundant. But speculation seems to have gone no further than this, and probably for the good reason that Leighton and Adelaide were, in fact, just friends and never lovers. Adelaide was extravagantly affectionate toward him, but she was this way with several male confidants outside her marriage. Chief among them, even ahead of Leighton, was the homosexual Henry Greville, a polished man about town and keen amateur singer for whom she had named her elder son. For his part, Leighton seems to have put all his sexual feelings into his art, much of which is unashamedly sensuous, and acted so little upon his inclinations that it is impossible to tell for sure what they were. Despite his flirting with Henry Greville and lack of enthusiasm for marriage, he was not necessarily homosexual. If he was, he may not have been exclusively so, and later appears to have had an illegitimate son with one of his models, Lily Mason.[22] In any case, it is fairly clear that his feeling for Adelaide was one of fond admiration rather than physical attraction. In a letter of February 19, 1855, he wrote to his mother, disingenuously or not, that Adelaide may have spoiled him for marriage: "I look upon her as an angel, *ni plus ni moins*, and I feel terrified at the idea of how much more exacting she has made me for the future choice of a wife, by showing one what opposite excellencies a woman may unite in herself."[23] Later Adelaide herself would encourage him, in vain, to take an interest in younger women: "Oh Fay, wouldn't she do?"[24]

The nickname "Fay," which Adelaide used for Leighton throughout their friendship, seems to have arisen in nursery talk. The Sartorises had three children: Greville Edward, who was nine when Leighton first met them; Mary Theodosia, who was seven—her middle name was a tribute to Adelaide's friend Theodosia Monson; and Algernon Charles, an eighteen-month-old baby. As Mrs. Russell Barrington noted, the artist became attached to the young Sartorises as to their mother: "The Sartoris children were another source of delight to Leighton in this home. No greater child-lover ever existed."[25] Soon he was making drawings of them (fig. 5). Adelaide called Greville "Gay" and Mary "May," so to call their friend Frederic "Fay" would have come naturally enough. In her novel *A Week in a French Country-House*, she would use Leighton as the model for the character of Monsieur Kiowski, a young artist, and draw on memories of his unexpected interest and pleasure in children. "Mothers and children seemed to be favourite subjects with him," the novel's narrator, Bessie Hope,

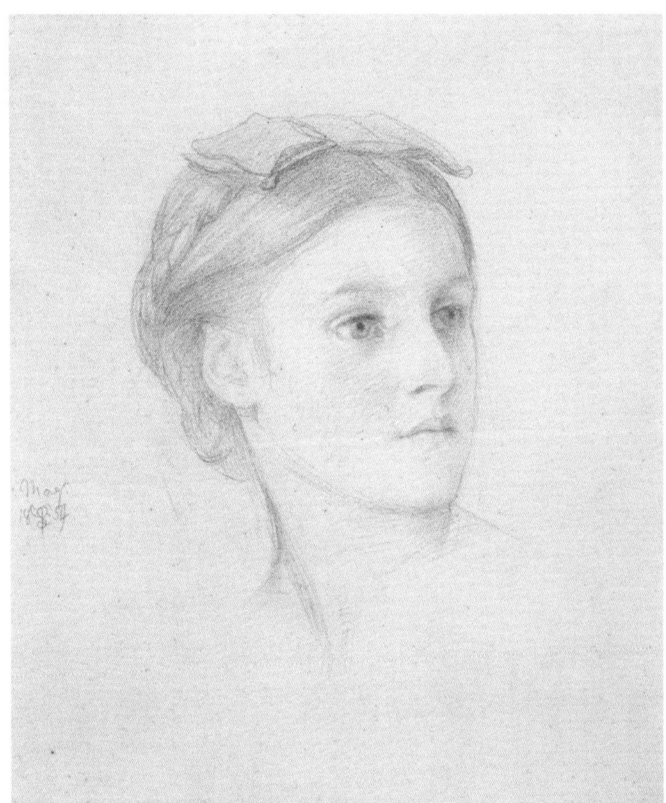

Fig. 5. Frederic Leighton, *May Sartoris,* 1854. Pencil, 7⅞ x 6¾ in. (20 x 17.2 cm). Bolton Museum

observes of Kiowski. "His book was filled with children in every sort of position: his babies are perfect,—so unconscious, and all the little lovely melting bits—the round of the temple and cheek, the little soft way in which the head sits on the neck of a baby—felt with a maternal tenderness that seemed quite extraordinary in a young man."[26] Leighton's mother once saw him holding a baby and felt all the more disappointed by his apparent indifference about marriage. She wrote to his sister: "For my part, it gave me actual pain to see that proof of his strong love of children, believing that he will never have any of his own. He declares he has never seen a girl he could marry. Of course this shows he is unreasonably fastidious; more's the pity!"[27]

Adelaide's son Algernon was an exceptionally pretty little boy—certainly Leighton thought so—and he was the first member of the family with whom he went beyond pencil

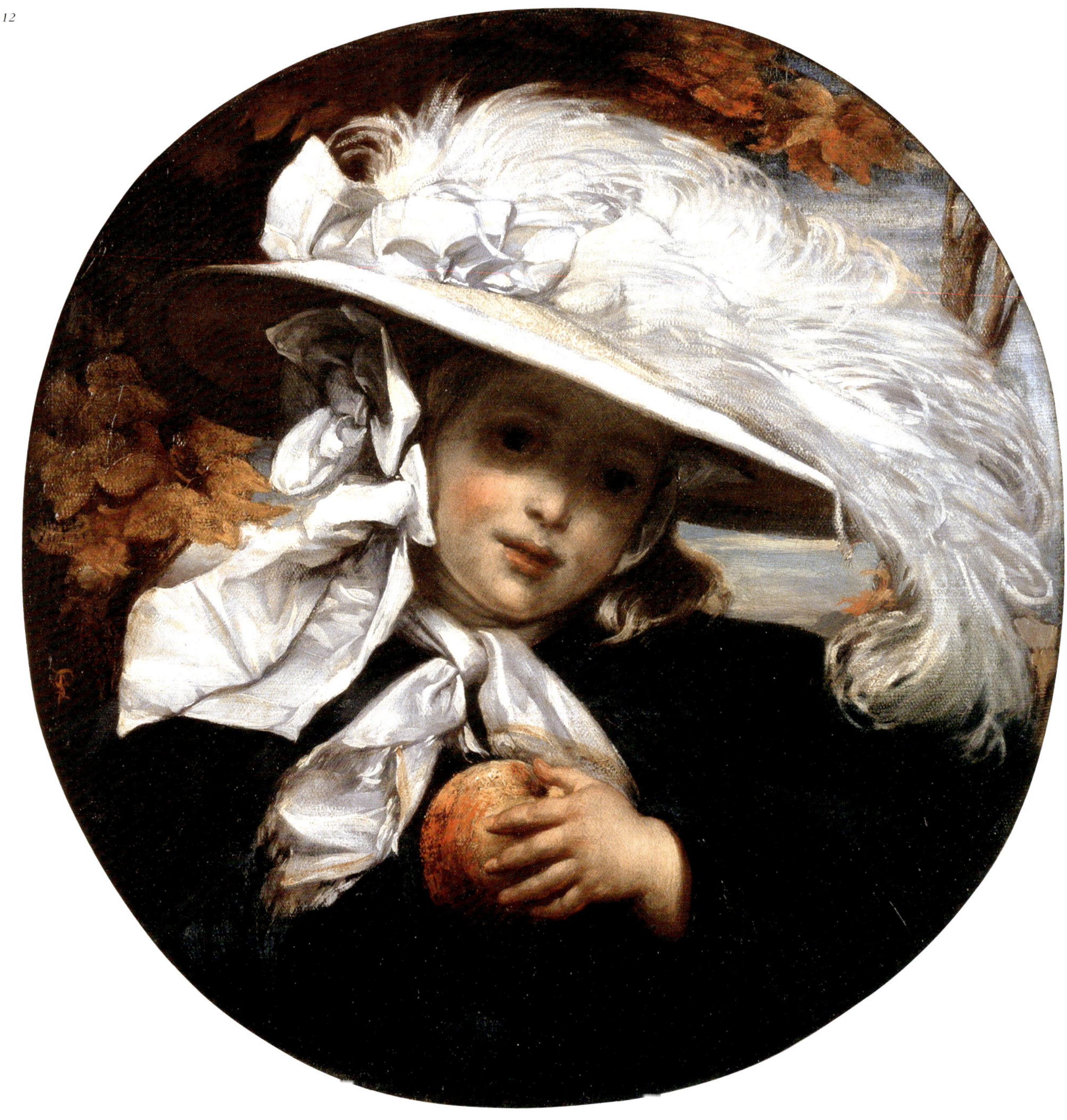

Fig. 6. Frederic Leighton, *Algernon Sartoris*, c. 1853–54. Oil on canvas, diam. approx. 19½ in. (49.5 cm). Private collection

sketches and made a painted portrait (fig. 6). "Little baby is the same sunbeam that he always was," he wrote in a letter from Rome, probably to his mother. "Did I tell you I painted his likeness in oils as a surprise for his father? As a picture it is not unsuccessful, but any attempt at a portrait of that child is a profanation, and will be till we paint with the down of peaches and the blood of cherries, and mix our tints with golden sunlight; still, it pleased *them*, and that ought to be enough; but I am an artist as well as a friend."[28] In the portrait Algernon is holding an apple rather than a peach or cherries, but the idea is the same—the artist invites us to compare his rosy cheeks with the colors in the fruit. It was not uncommon for Victorian mothers to put boys in outfits that to modern eyes look girlish, but Algernon's feathered hat, ribbons, and bows are an extreme case. One can only imagine how it must have embarrassed him in later life. His misfortune was to have a mother for whom all kinds of theatricality, including dressing up in extravagant costumes, were second nature. In this element of "fancy dress," as in the feathered hat and elaborate cap in particular, the work was a forerunner of the portrait of Algernon's sister, May, that the artist would paint in England. Leighton seems never to have painted Algernon again, although there is a later pencil sketch of him that shows off his long hair (fig. 7).

Though mainly a painter of historical subjects, and destined to win acclaim for his evocations of ancient Greece as a world of beauty and refinement, Leighton enjoyed painting portraits, especially portraits of people he liked as much as the Sartorises. Having finished his great *Cimabue's Madonna*, he began to think about painting a portrait of Adelaide herself, one that would further express the friendship and gratitude he felt toward her and her family. On February 10, 1855, he wrote to his father of his reasons for staying on in Rome: "I do not hesitate to say, the principal task which I propose to myself is a half-length portrait of Mrs. Sartoris, to which I wish to devote my every energy that it may be worthy of perpetuating the features of the last Kemble; irrespective of the enormous artistic advantage to be derived from the study of so exceptional a head, you will easily understand my eagerness to give some tangible form to my gratitude towards those whose fireside has been my fireside for so long a time; nothing would grieve me more than missing such a good opportunity."[29] By March 2, when he wrote from Rome to his sister, he was considering his friend's looks very much with a portraitist's eye: "She is the image of John Kemble, with large aquiline nose

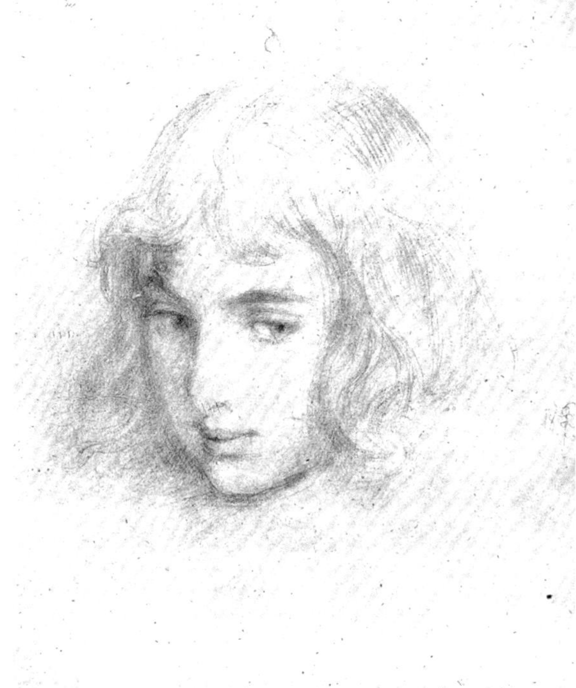

Fig. 7. Frederic Leighton, *Algernon Sartoris*, 1855. Pencil, 7¼ x 6 in. (18.3 x 15.2 cm). Private collection

and the most beautiful mouth in the world, a most harmonious head, and, like Fanny, the hair low down on her forehead; artistically speaking, her head and shoulders are the finest I ever saw with the exception only of Dante's; in spite of all this, many people think her barely good-looking, because she has no complexion, very little hair, and is excessively stout."[30]

The idea of painting a Kemble, a member of the first family of the British theater, must have been doubly exciting in that Leighton knew he was following in the footsteps of some of the most celebrated British artists of the past. Both Joshua Reynolds and Thomas Gainsborough painted Adelaide's aunt Sarah Siddons, each in a way that typifies his approach to portraiture. Reynolds showed her as the Tragic Muse, Gainsborough as a lady of fashion.[31] Both artists brought out that most salient point of family iconography, the Kemble nose, and Gainsborough felt he had to struggle to keep it from dominating the whole portrait, exclaiming "Confound the nose, there's no end to it!"[32] When Leighton mentioned Adelaide's resemblance to her uncle John Philip Kemble, he probably had in mind the great portraits of the actor by Thomas Lawrence, especially the one showing him in the role of Hamlet, then at the National Gallery in London (fig. 8). Lawrence painted Mrs. Siddons too, and his last portrait of her, a full-length, was also at the National Gallery (fig. 9). Lawrence had a long and intimate friendship with Siddons, not unlike Leighton's friendship with Adelaide; he was reputedly engaged to one of her daughters, although they never married, and in love with another. In the portraits at the National Gallery he showed Siddons and her brother in full face—in this case playing down the Kemble nose—and associated both with the tragic colors of red and black, suggestive of blood and death. Lawrence painted and drew other members of the family, and Adelaide apparently owned drawings by him of both her father and her sister.[33]

Later in the same letter of March 2, 1855, Leighton told his sister that he had begun painting not only Adelaide but also her daughter, now aged nine or ten: "I shall send you soon two photographs of portraits that I am now painting; one of Mrs. Sartoris, the other of her little daughter May."[34] Unfortunately, no such photographs have come down, nor does there appear to be any further record of the portraits themselves. Leighton may or may not have completed them, and the absence of any trace of their existence beyond his letters to his father and sister suggests that he probably did not. It remains a possibility that he began painting May in Rome in 1855 and finished her portrait in England some years later, the Roman portrait and the canvas in the Kimbell Art Museum being one and the same. But, on balance, they seem much more likely to have been separate projects, especially considering the obvious problems involved in painting a child's likeness over an extended period of time. If Leighton had indeed finished the work so long after beginning it, one would expect to see major changes to the face, figure, or background, but none are apparent, either to the naked eye or in X-radiographs.

In the summer of 1855 Leighton showed his great painting of *Cimabue's Madonna* at the Royal Academy's annual exhibition in London and sold it to no less an admirer than Queen Victoria. He had made his name at home, and some must have expected him to make the most of his success by settling in London. But still he preferred to live abroad, and by the end of the year had taken a studio in Paris—at 21, rue Pigalle. No doubt he made his plans in concert with the Sartorises, and that November they too moved to Paris. For the next three years

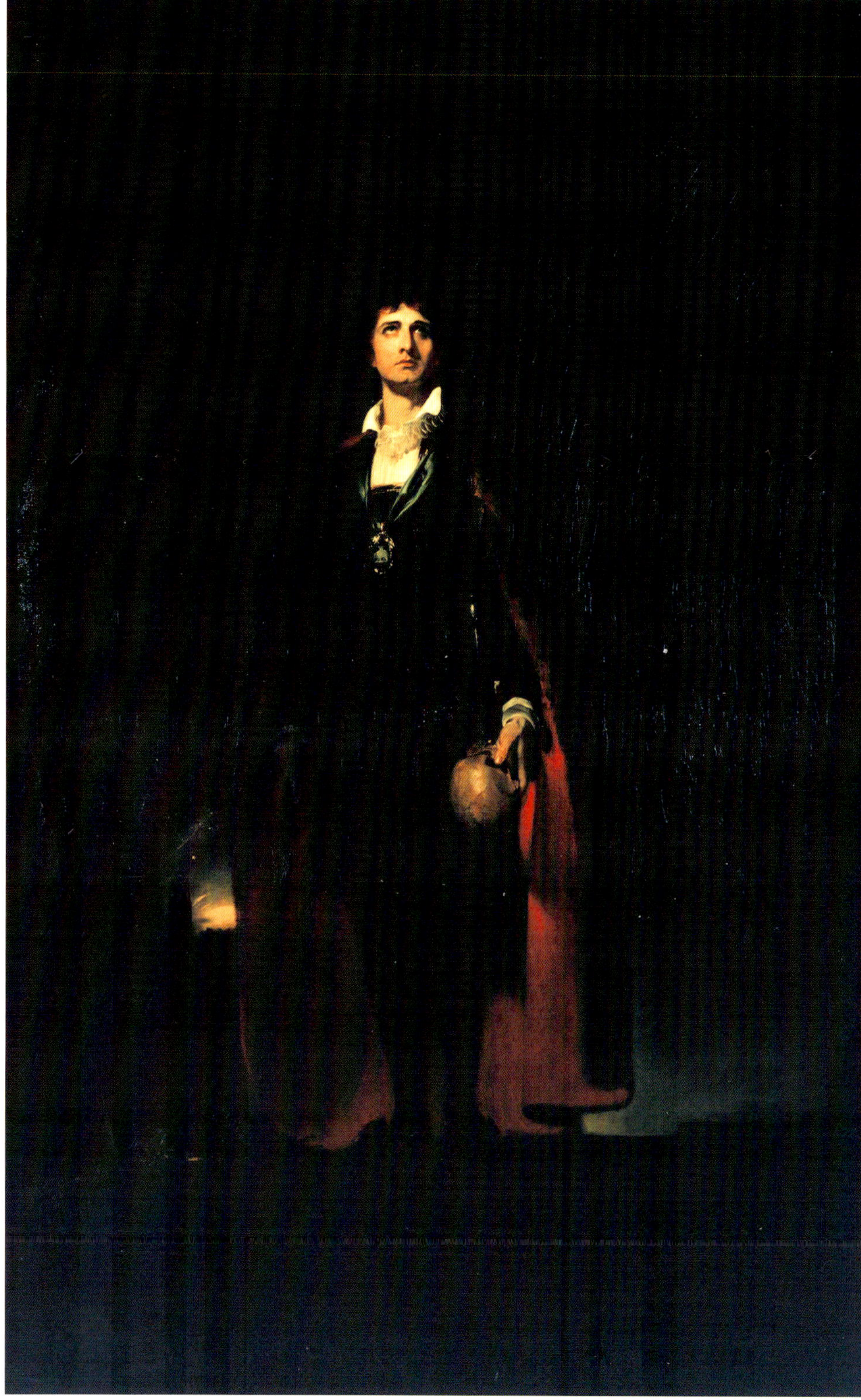

Fig. 8. Thomas Lawrence, *John Philip Kemble as Hamlet*, 1801. Oil on canvas, 120½ x 78 in. (306.1 x 198.1 cm). Tate, London

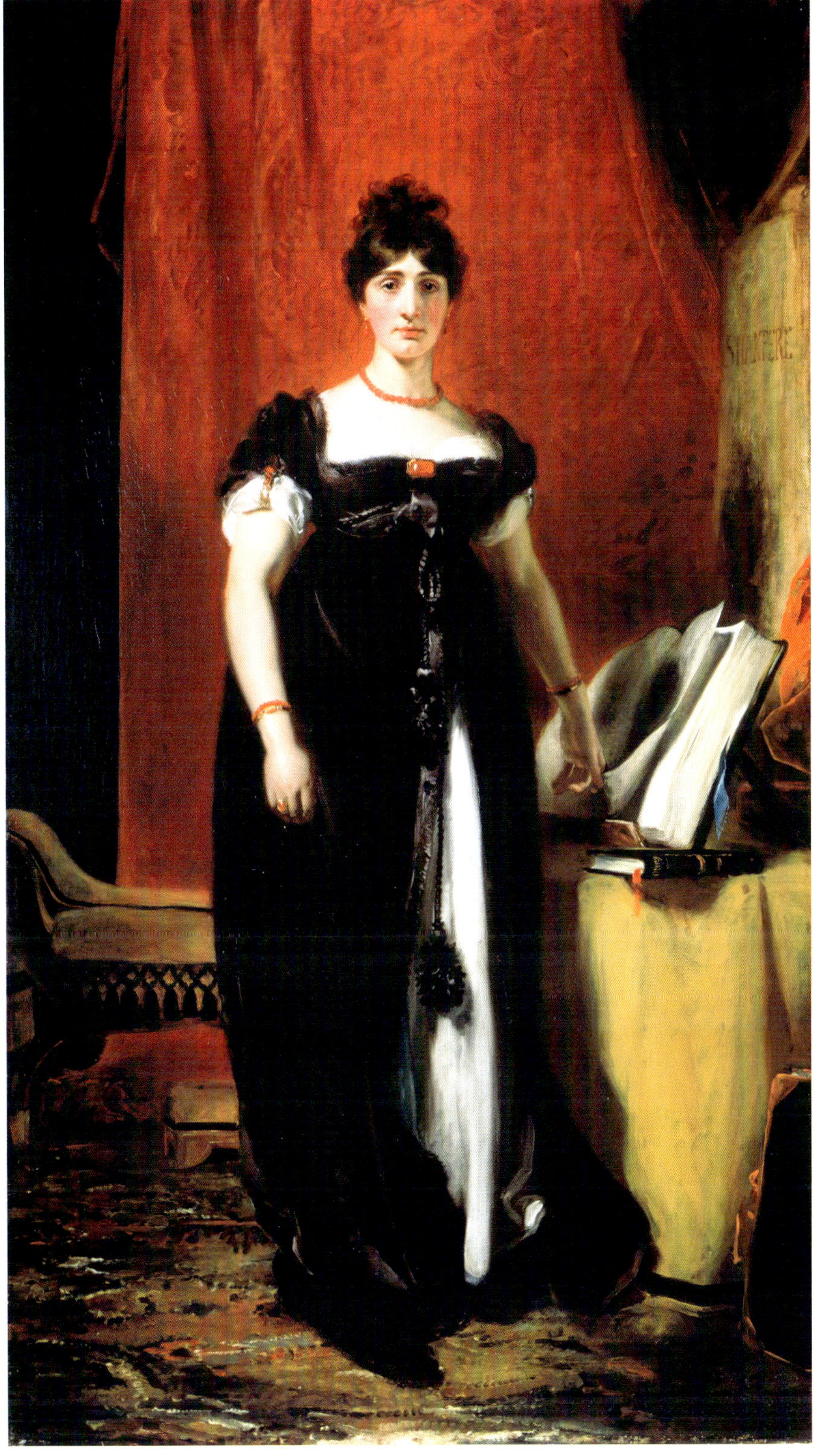

Fig. 9. Thomas Lawrence, *Sarah Siddons*, 1804.
Oil on canvas, 100 x 58¼ in. (254 x 148.1 cm). Tate, London

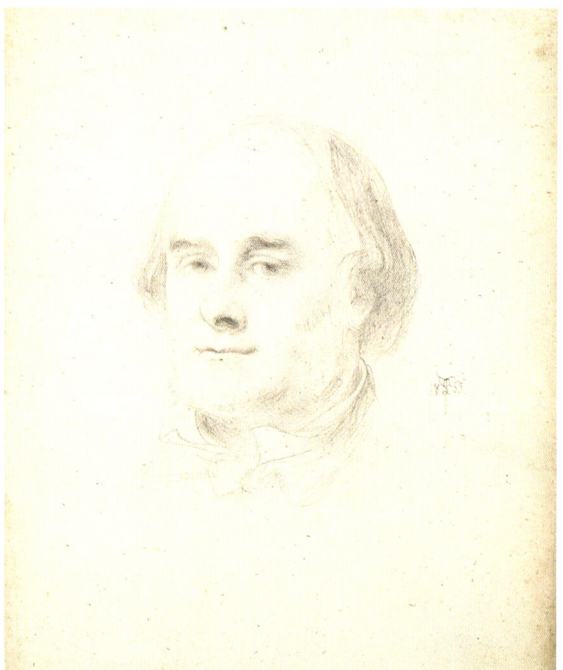

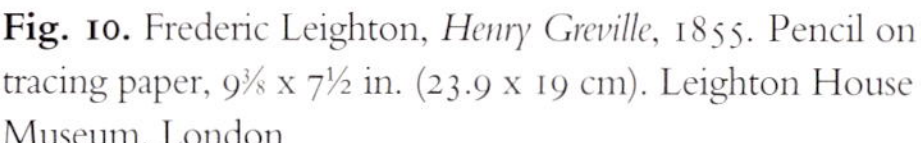

Fig. 10. Frederic Leighton, *Henry Greville*, 1855. Pencil on tracing paper, 9⅜ x 7½ in. (23.9 x 19 cm). Leighton House Museum, London

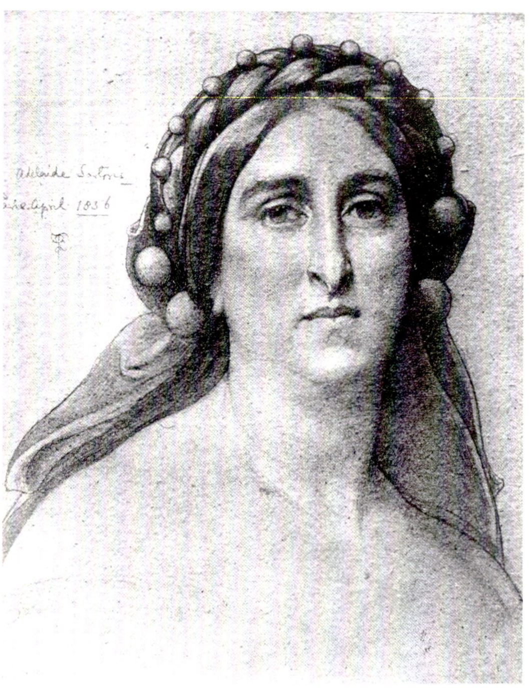

Fig. 11. Frederic Leighton, *Adelaide Sartoris*, 1856. Pencil drawing. Present whereabouts unknown. Reproduced from Mrs. Russell Barrington, *The Life, Letters and Work of Frederic Leighton*, London, 1906

and more, albeit intermittently since they all traveled so much, Leighton and the Sartorises lived a Parisian version of the social life they had enjoyed in Rome, taking every opportunity to gather together members of the old Roman circle, including the Brownings. Leighton saw more of Adelaide's beloved Henry Greville, and they became close friends (fig. 10).

It was in Paris in April 1856, presumably in the apartment that the Sartorises leased in the rue Royale, that Leighton made his fullest known portrait of Adelaide, a pencil drawing (fig. 11). This may give some idea of the appearance of the now-lost painting of her that he began in Rome about a year earlier, although the attention paid to the details of high fashion, especially in the hair dressing, seems distinctively Parisian. In this respect and in the unabashed plumpness of Adelaide's figure, the drawing recalls the portraits of Ingres. It is particularly close to the earlier of the two portraits of Madame Paul-Sigisbert Moitessier (fig. 12).[35] Leighton would have seen this when he visited the Paris Exposition Universelle of 1855, which included a special display of Ingres's works.

Fig. 12. Jean-Auguste-Dominique Ingres, *Madame Moitessier*, 1851. Oil on canvas, 57¾ x 39⅜ in. (147 x 100 cm). National Gallery of Art, Washington, D.C., Samuel H. Kress Collection

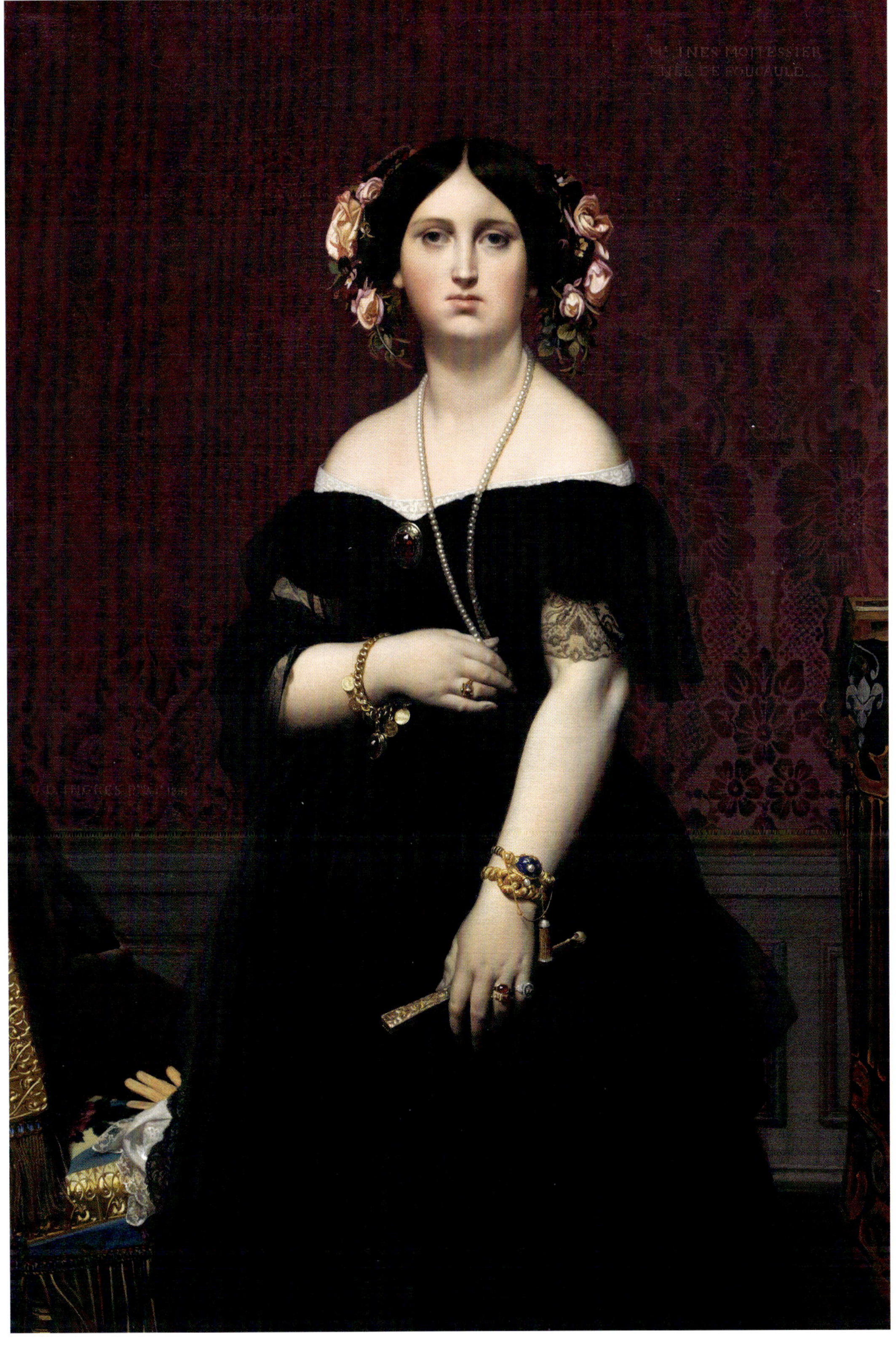

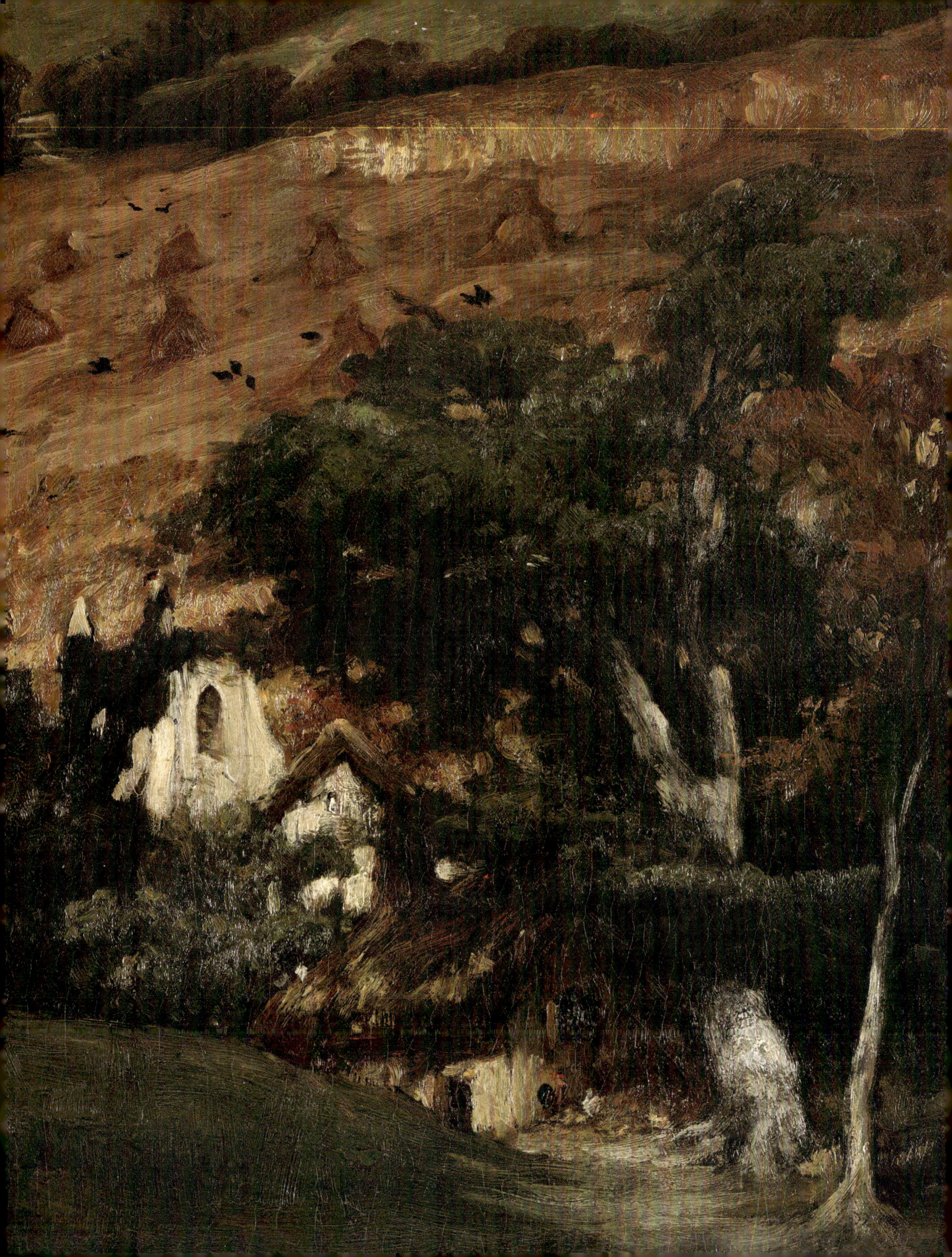

An English Portrait

IN 1859 LEIGHTON FINALLY BROUGHT HIS EXPATRIATE EXISTENCE TO AN END AND CAME to live in London, where he would spend most of his time and do most of his work for the rest of his life. He took a house and studio at 2 Orme Square in Bayswater, on the north side of Kensington Gardens. "Of course after Paris and Rome it is a sad falling-off," he wrote to his mother, "narrow and dark, though I believe, for London, very fair."[36] Again the move seems to have been coordinated with the Sartorises, who duly left Paris, stayed for a time in London, then settled in the countryside near Petersfield in Hampshire, about fifty miles southwest of London and therefore within fairly easy visiting distance (see fig. 16). Their new residence was Westbury House, a stately Palladian mansion leased from Henry, 4th Viscount Gage, of Firle Place in Sussex (fig. 14).[37] The approach to the house was along a tree-lined drive off the road between the villages of East Meon and West Meon. The drive looped into an oval on the north side of the house, and on the south side were pleasure grounds designed by the celebrated early eighteenth-century landscape gardener Charles Bridgman (fig. 15). Surrounding the house and gardens was a working estate with a farmyard, barns and stables, fields and timber plantations. The family's connection to this particular part of the country was through a maternal uncle of Edward Sartoris's named Edward Tunno, who lived nearby at Warnford Park and whose sizeable fortune Sartoris stood to inherit.

Fig. 13. Frederic Leighton, *May Sartoris*, detail (see fig. 19)

Adelaide and Edward entertained regularly at Westbury, and Leighton was a frequent guest. "The Sartoris, you know, are no longer in London—a great loss to all their friends," he wrote to Robert Browning on January 29, 1860, "but I go pretty often to see them in the country, and have spent many a happy day there in the course of the winter."[38] He described life at Westbury and reported family news in a number of letters to Adelaide's sister, Fanny, then living unhappily in Boston and Lenox, Massachusetts. He told her about the Christmas festivities at the house, about a drawing room redecorated in red velvet that Fanny imagined must be "very becoming to the pictures," about some sketching he had been doing.[39] He sent her one of his Westbury sketches, and she was keenly nostalgic, writing to him on March 15, 1860: "Dear Mr. Leighton, thank you a thousand times for the *portrait* of Westbury—it is exactly what I wished for—but, oh, why could there not be the lovely upland beyond, and the sheep slowly rolling up and down the slopes, and the tinkle of the bell, and you and she and they and all of us. Oh dear, if you could conceive what it is to me to be *here*, you would know a thousand times better than I can tell you how precious such a memento of *there* is to me."[40] Landscape had not played a large part in Leighton's art to date, but on a visit to Capri in the spring and summer of 1859 he had made the first of his exquisite landscape oil sketches.[41] It is impossible to tell whether his sketches at Westbury were oil sketches or drawings; unfortunately, neither the one he sent Fanny Kemble nor any other has been traced.

Not long after the Sartorises settled in at Westbury, Leighton painted the portrait of May now at the Kimbell, the most important expression of his affection and gratitude toward the family (fig. 19). May was a petite fourteen- or fifteen-year-old at the time. Only one preparatory sketch for her portrait is known, a roughing-out of the composition on a page in a sketchbook (fig. 18), but at least part of the artist's purpose in making the sketches around Westbury that he mentioned to Fanny Kemble may have been to gather material for a landscape background that conveyed the character and beauty of the Meon Valley. He may have sketched near Marland's Mill, a windmill on a hill about a mile and a half northwest of the house, and this local landmark was perhaps the basis for the inclusion of a windmill in the upper-left corner of the portrait (fig. 17). The painted windmill resembles the actual one only in the broadest sense, however—and the apparently ruined church on the right, with

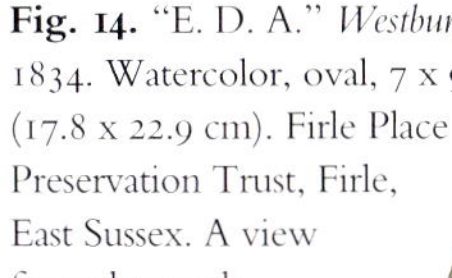

Fig. 14. "E. D. A." *Westbury*, 1834. Watercolor, oval, 7 x 9 in. (17.8 x 22.9 cm). Firle Place Preservation Trust, Firle, East Sussex. A view from the south

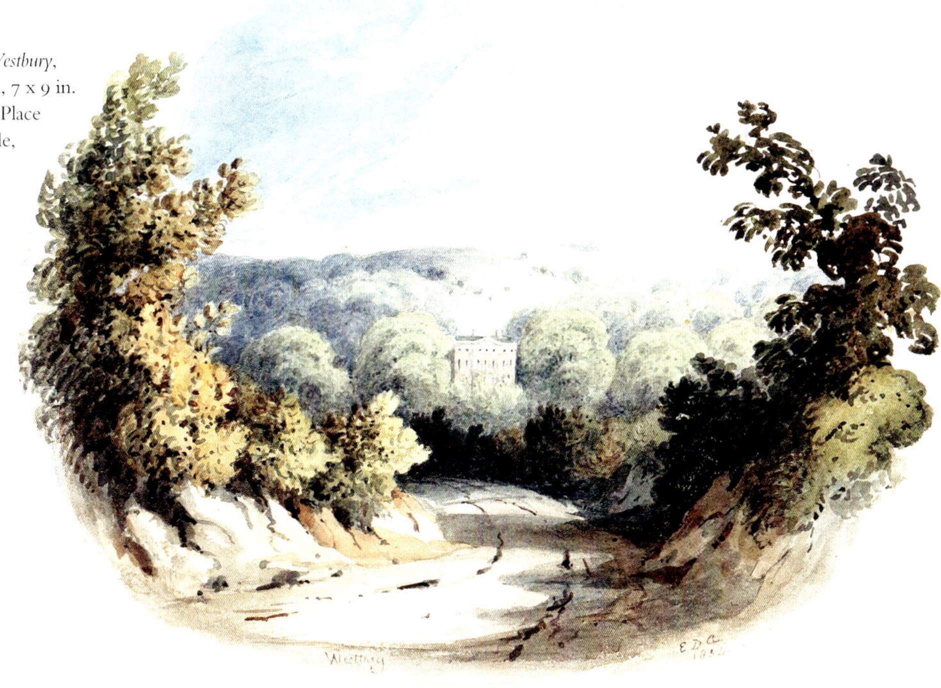

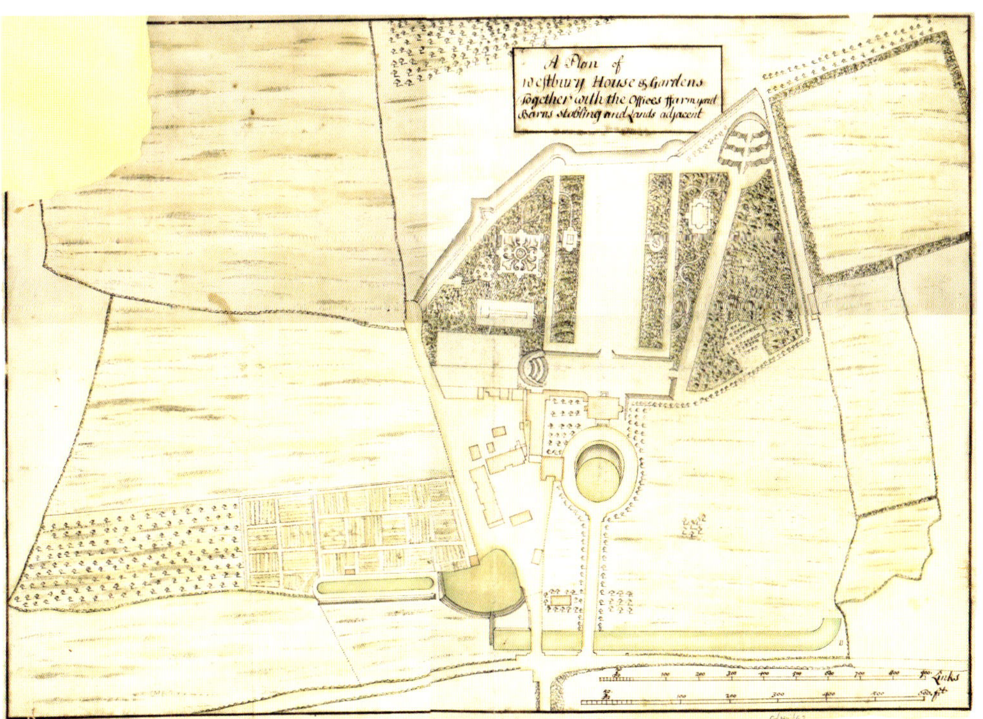

Fig. 15. *A Plan of Westbury House & Gardens . . . etc.*, 1761. Ink and watercolor, 21 x 29½ in. (53.3 x 74.9 cm). East Sussex Record Office, Lewes. Oriented with the south at the top

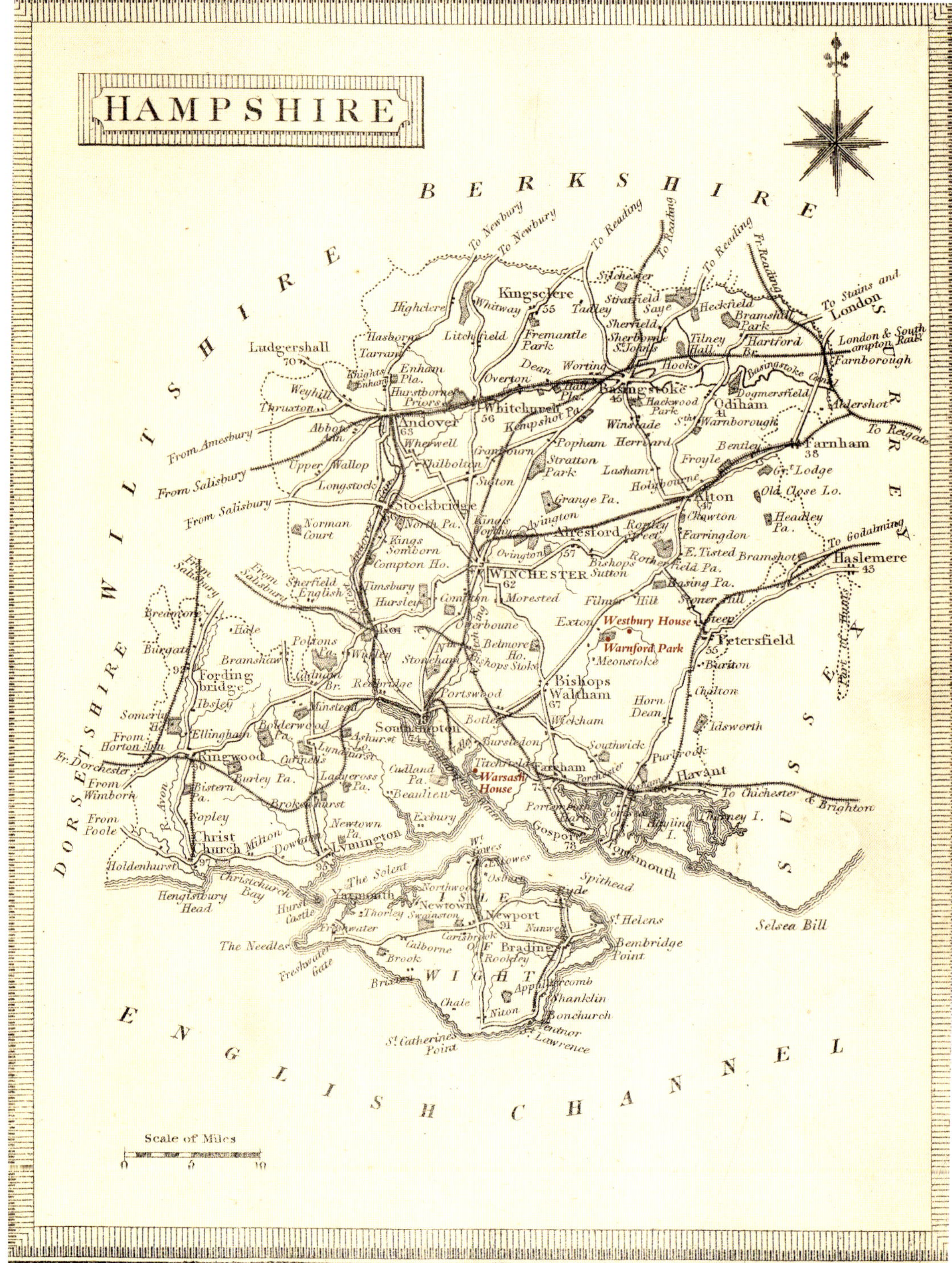

Fig. 16. Map of Hampshire, 1860s, showing residences of the Sartoris family

its dilapidated, ivy-covered steeple, is similarly generic (fig. 13). The forms of the hills seem to belong to this part of Hampshire yet elude identification as any particular view. As we might expect from an artist well grounded in the classical principle of the Ideal, Leighton seems to have been out to capture the spirit of the place not the letter, and felt free to alter and reorganize topography to suit his purposes. The Sartorises may well have encouraged him in this, preferring to see May in a generalized Hampshire setting rather than a specific Westbury one. They were only renting Westbury, after all, and knew that before long they would move somewhere else. There is no way of knowing whether Leighton painted the portrait at Westbury or in his London studio; he may have worked on it in either or perhaps both places.

Both Leighton and the Sartorises were back in England after years of living mainly in Italy and France, and the portrait of May seems in different ways, not least its greenness, to show a vision of home typical of the returning expatriate. Adelaide was to draw upon the experience of seeing England as greener and pleasanter than ever after being abroad in the opening scene of her unfinished story *Judith*, describing the return of Richard Leslie to Brankleigh Manor House:

> After a three-years' sojourn in the south of Italy, the sight of the dewy pastures, the grand old trees, and all the wonderful freshness of the English green, filled our traveler with delight. The whole road down from London had seemed to him one uninterrupted well-ordered garden; and the air of peace and well-being, the prosperity of the whole landscape, brought the young man to his journey's end with a sensation of satisfaction in the land to which he belonged, and to himself for belonging to it, not altogether unknown to Britons, travelled and untravelled.[42]

The portrait of May is the most English of all Leighton's paintings, not only in setting but also in its relationship to English artistic traditions. Until now, he had been essentially a Continental artist, and there remains something of a foreign accent about the work—an Ingres-like perfection about the face that Millais, for instance, would have found unnatural and lacking in character, an approach to the painting of landscape more akin to the Barbizon school than to Constable, Turner, or the Pre-Raphaelites.[43] Still, there was no genre of

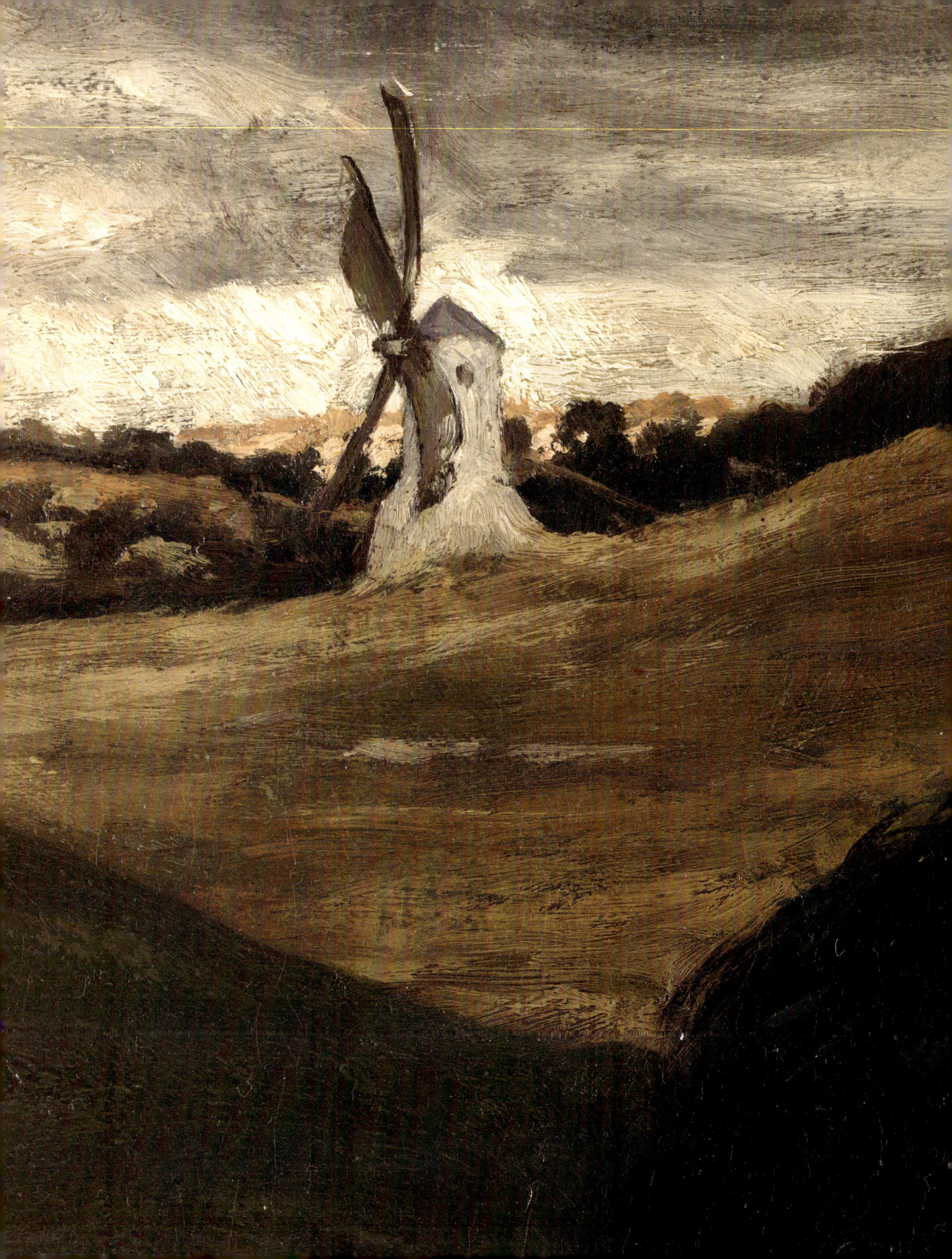

Fig. 18. Frederic Leighton, Sketch for *May Sartoris*, c. 1860. Pencil, 6½ x 4⅛ (16.6 x 10.4 cm), in a sketchbook. Royal Academy of Arts, London

painting more closely associated with England than child portraiture in an outdoor setting, and the staging of May's portrait is an unmistakable homage to English child portraitists of the eighteenth and early nineteenth centuries.

The most beloved and esteemed of these was the founding president of the Royal Academy, Joshua Reynolds. Like Leighton, Reynolds never married. He had no children

Fig. 17. Frederic Leighton, *May Sartoris*, detail (see fig. 19)

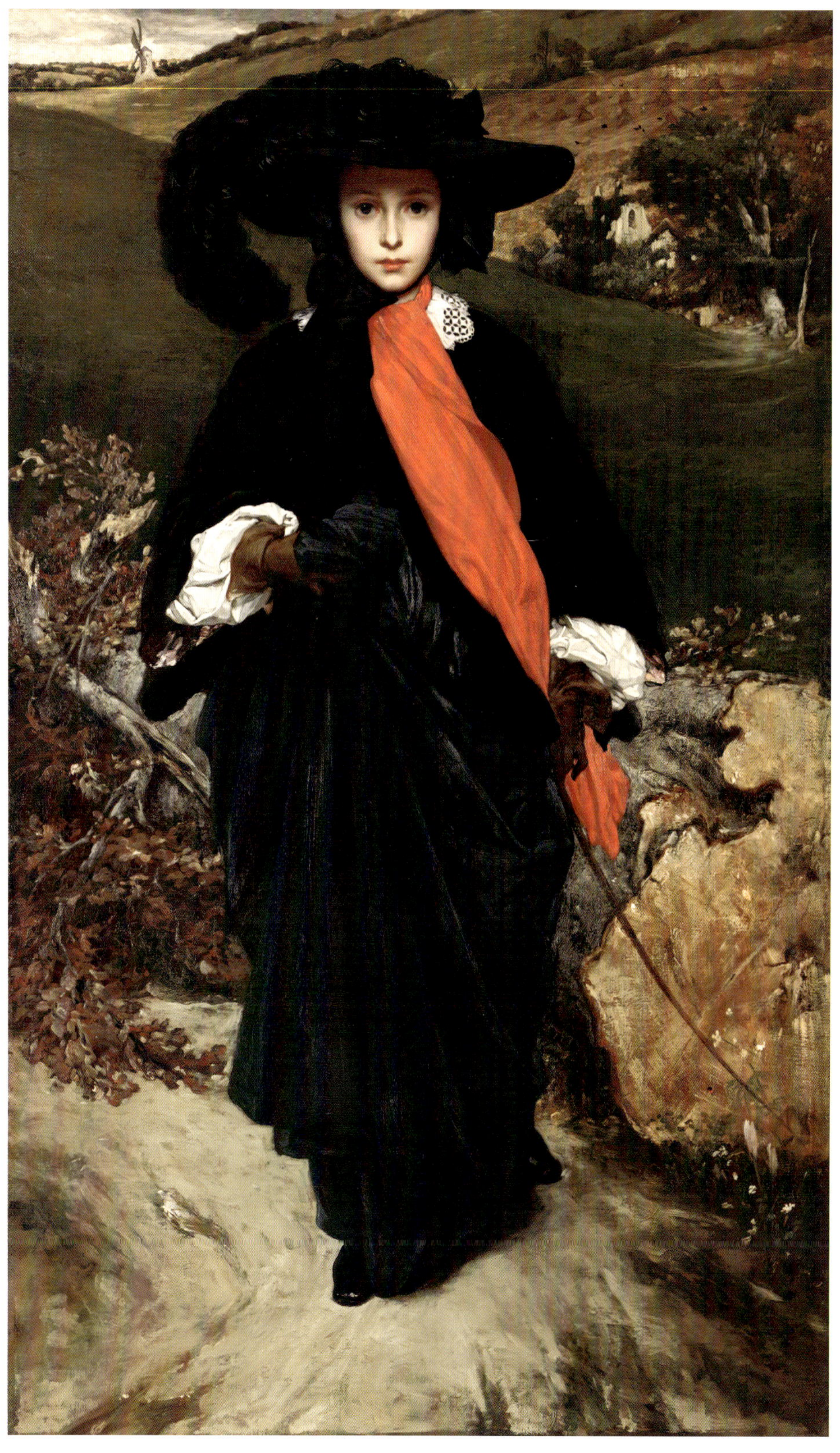

of his own, but to his Victorian admirers this made his sensitivity as a painter of childhood all the more remarkable. "It must have occurred to the minds of many among my readers," wrote the critic F. G. Stephens, "that Reynolds, of all artists, painted children best—that the childless man knew most of childhood, depicted its appearances in the truest and happiest spirit of comedy, entered into its changeful soul with the tenderest, heartiest sympathy, played with the playful, sighed with the sorrowful, and mastered all the craft of infancy."[44] When he composed May's portrait, Leighton may well have had in mind, as a model of English child portraiture at its most delightful, Reynolds's famous portrait of Lady Caroline Scott (fig. 20). He may never have seen the work at first hand but would certainly have known it through engraved reproductions.

Among the great English child portraitists of the past, he would also have been especially conscious of Thomas Lawrence, who painted May's great-uncle John Philip Kemble and her great-aunt Sarah Siddons. He probably knew Lawrence's *Pinkie*, a portrait of the eleven-year-old Sarah Goodin Barrett Moulton (fig. 21). His friend Elizabeth Barrett Browning had grown up with *Pinkie* as a family portrait, and it now belonged to her brother Charles.[45] Perhaps Leighton used it as another of the English child portraits of the past to play off as he conceived his portrait of May. Certainly it seems possible when we consider the two together: they would work well as a complementary pair, the Lawrence suggesting the mirthful, active side of childhood, the Leighton suggesting a melancholy, contemplative side. Among portraits of his own time, Leighton may have been responding in particular to Francis Grant's portrait of his daughter, a latter-day variation on the theme of Reynolds's portrait of Lady Caroline Scott that had been in the Royal Academy exhibition of 1857 (fig. 22). Certainly Adelaide knew Grant, who had painted her in her youth, and perhaps the portrait of his daughter came up as she discussed the portrait of her own daughter with Leighton.

Adelaide's surviving letters give just a few glimpses of May's personality. She was so "healthy, happy, reasonable, affectionate, and helpful" that her mother wondered "whether I really did bring her into the world."[46] Whereas her older brother Greville was like their not especially dynamic father, May had energy and determination, "more like *me*."[47] If

Fig. 19. Frederic Leighton, *May Sartoris*, c. 1860. Oil on canvas, 59⅞ x 35½ in. (152.1 x 90.2 cm). Kimbell Art Museum, Fort Worth

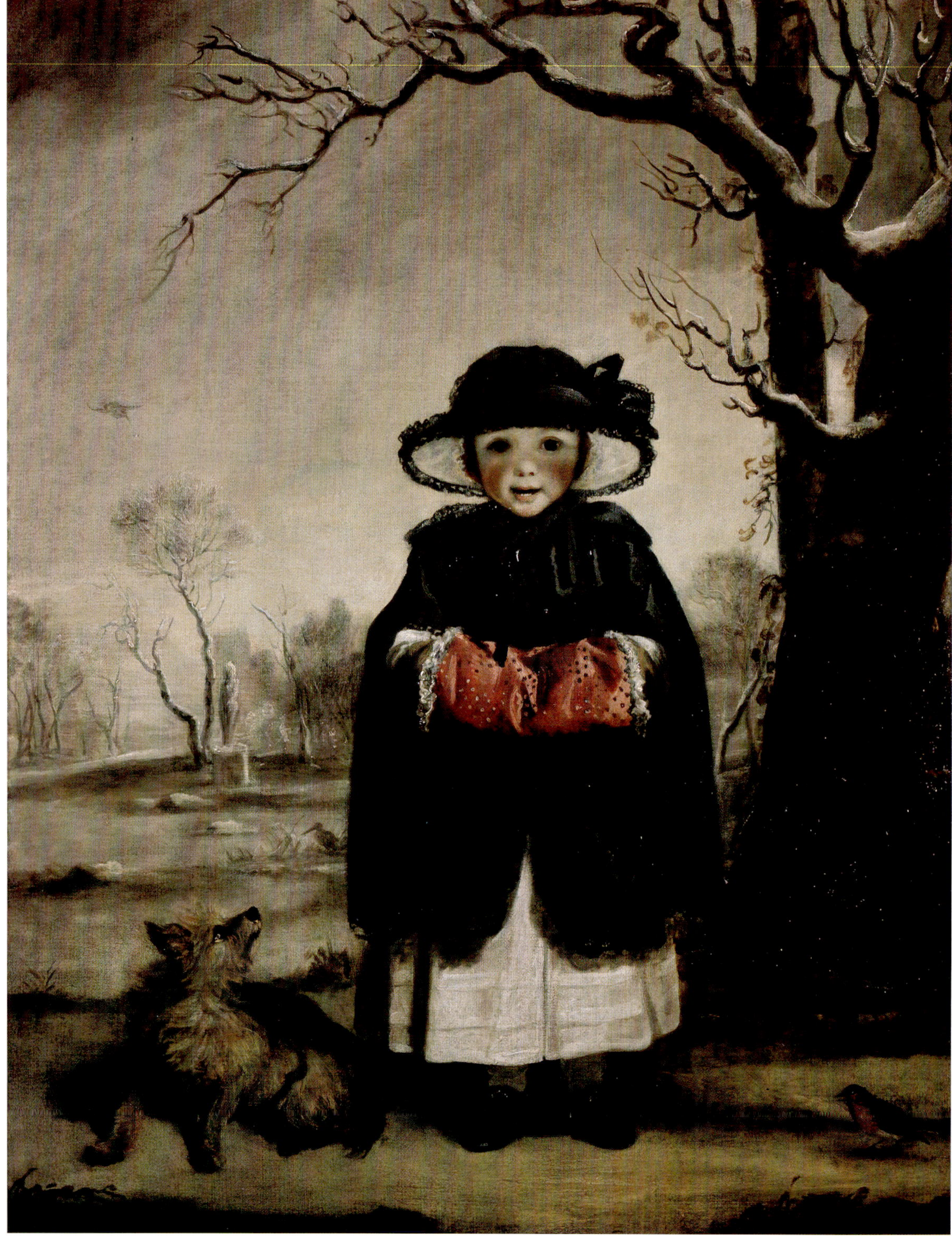

Fig. 20. Joshua Reynolds, *Lady Caroline Scott as "Winter,"* 1776. Oil on canvas, 56½ x 44 in. (143.5 x 112 cm). His Grace the Duke of Buccleuch and Queensberry, KT

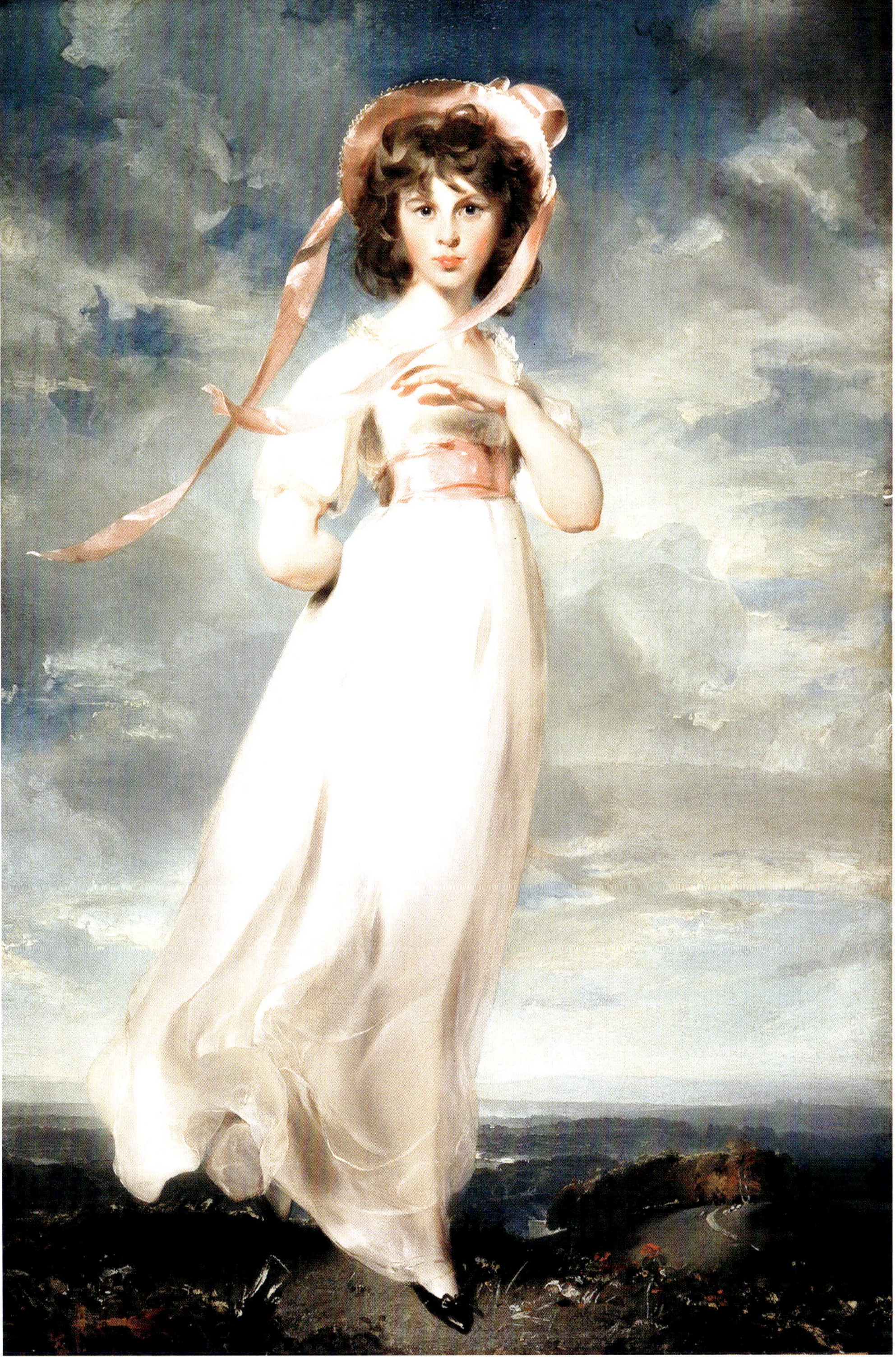

Fig. 21. Thomas Lawrence, *Sarah Goodin Barrett Moulton: "Pinkie,"* 1794. Oil on canvas, 58¼ x 40¼ in. (148 x 102.2 cm). The Huntington Library, Art Collections, and Botanical Gardens, San Marino, Calif.

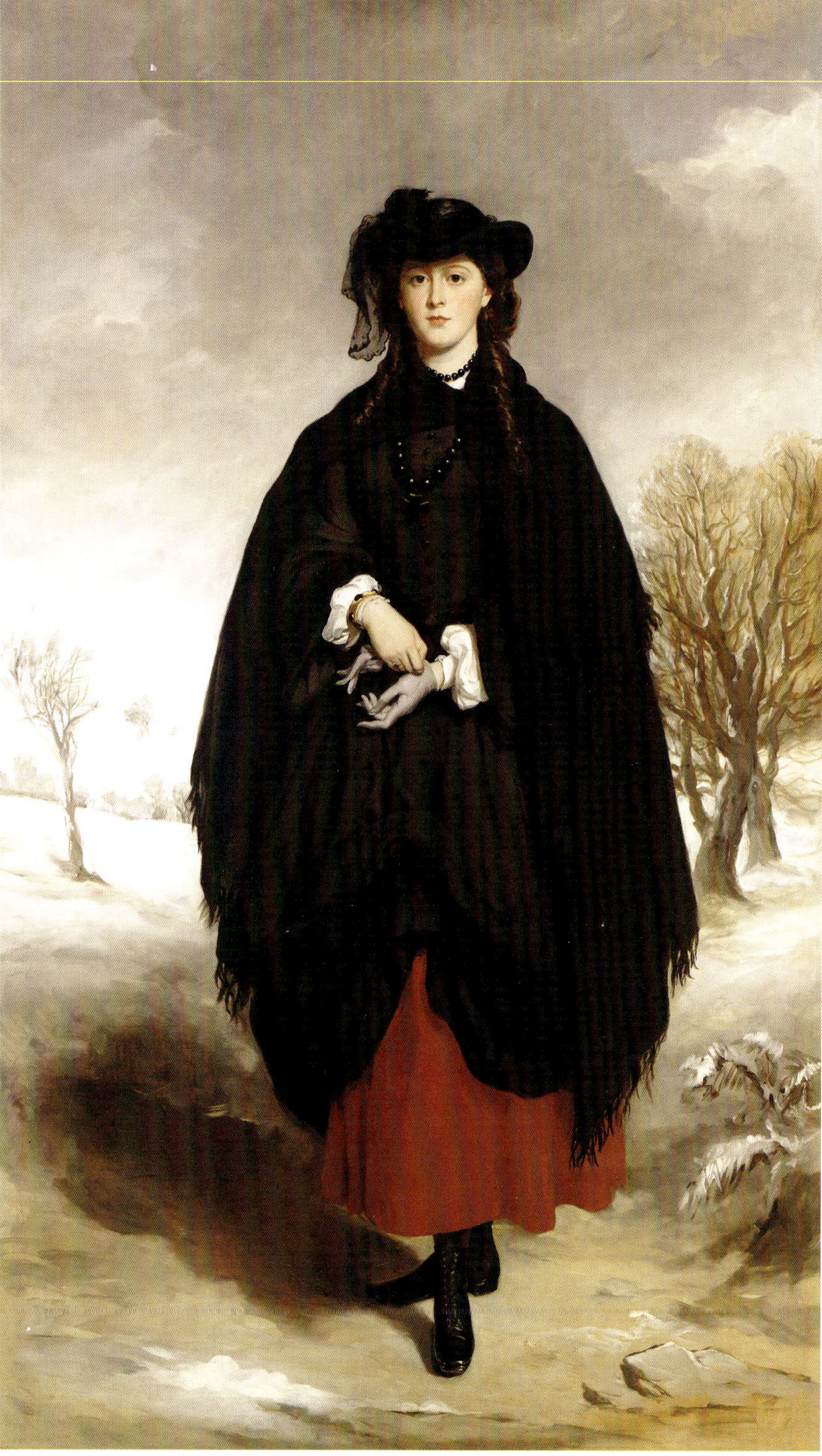

Fig. 22. Francis Grant, *Daisy Grant, Daughter of the Artist*, 1856–57. Oil on canvas, 88 x 52¼ in. (223.5 x 132.3 cm). Private collection

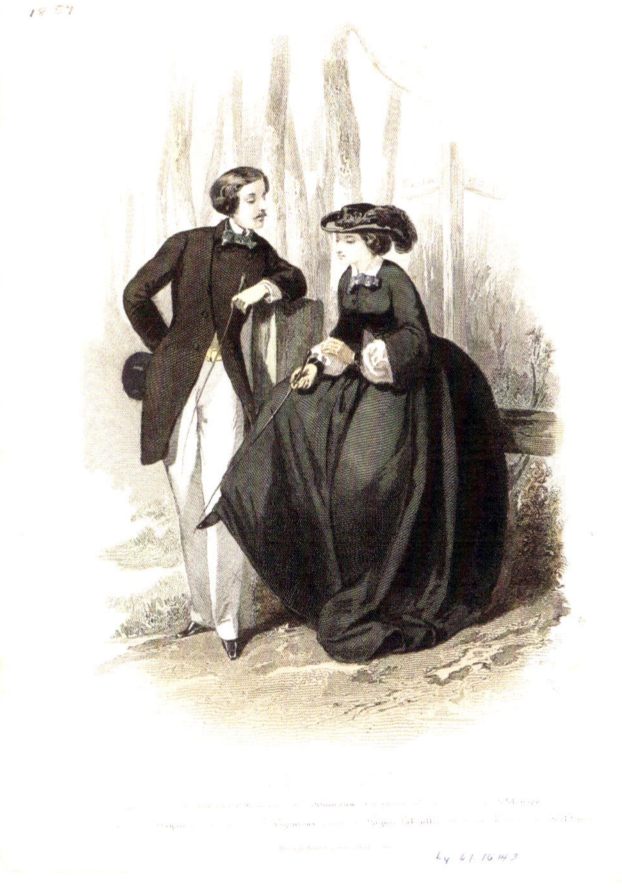

Fig. 23. Fashion plate from the series *Les Modes Parisiennes*, 1857. Engraving after François-Claudius Compte-Calix, with hand coloring, 10⅝ x 7¾ in. (26.9 x 19.7 cm). The Metropolitan Museum of Art, New York, The Irene Lewisohn Costume Reference Library, The Woodman Thompson Collection

May's Kemble side comes through in Leighton's portrait of her, as it seems to have come through in her character, it is most immediately in the way she is dressed. First, the dramatic red-black contrast of her scarf against her jacket harks back to the literally dramatic red-black portraits of John Philip Kemble and Mrs. Siddons by Lawrence. With its long skirts, her dark greenish blue dress seems to be a real riding habit of the time, indeed a fashionable one (see fig. 23). Her "pagoda" sleeves show a sartorial elegance befitting a Sartoris. But the way in which she wears a jacket over the riding habit, her collar of *broderie anglaise*, and above all her large, fanciful feathered hat—which, oddly, she wears on top of a cap—make her outfit seem more of a costume than clothing for a practical purpose. It is as though she were dressed for a performance of some kind, or maybe just for portrait-posing, in clothes that do not completely go together and are all a little too big for her, some perhaps borrowed from her mother. It was not uncommon for English portraitists to show children wearing oversized clothes, a way of bringing out their beguiling diminutiveness. In Leighton's case, however, the attraction of such a voluminous outfit, especially the skirts of the riding habit, was also that of drapery for drapery's sake. It is not only May who has so much dress that she has to pull it up in front of her in order to walk. So does Helen of Troy and other generously draped women in his later paintings of ancient Greek subjects.[48]

The mood of May's portrait is serious, even somber, for that of a child. Dressed in those mostly dark, heavy clothes and set against land rather than sky, she certainly does cut a different figure from the ethereal Pinkie, and in some respects the contrast typifies shifting ideas of childhood as presented in English art and literature. Between the Romantic girl and the Victorian girl, the joyful, carefree picture of childhood comes down to earth. May looks as if she might even be aware of this herself, feeling some vague but deep-seated sadness. Leighton's portrait joined countless other bittersweet Victorian images of children in which artists and writers dwelt on the idea of childhood, indeed life itself, as a passing thing. One of the most talked-about paintings at the Royal Academy's annual exhibition in 1856 was Millais's *Autumn Leaves*, a work that May's normally unforthcoming father Edward Sartoris saw there and said he liked (fig. 24).[49] Millais shows a group of girls solemnly building a bonfire of dead leaves. It is sunset, the dying time of the day, and the apple held by the girl on the right (who wears a bright red scarf) gently suggests the Fall of Man. The artist was almost certainly inspired, both in the subject of the painting and in its mood, by the poetry of Alfred Tennyson, especially his well-known song "Tears, idle tears" from *The Princess* (1847):

> Tears, idle tears, I know not what they mean,
> Tears from the depth of some divine despair
> Rise in the heart, and gather to the eyes,
> In looking on the happy Autumn-fields,
> And thinking of the days that are no more.[50]

Leighton also saw *Autumn Leaves* at the Royal Academy exhibition and may well have had this haunting image of the pathos of youth and innocence in his mind, consciously or not, when painting the portrait of May. It would be typical of his eclectic genius to draw not only

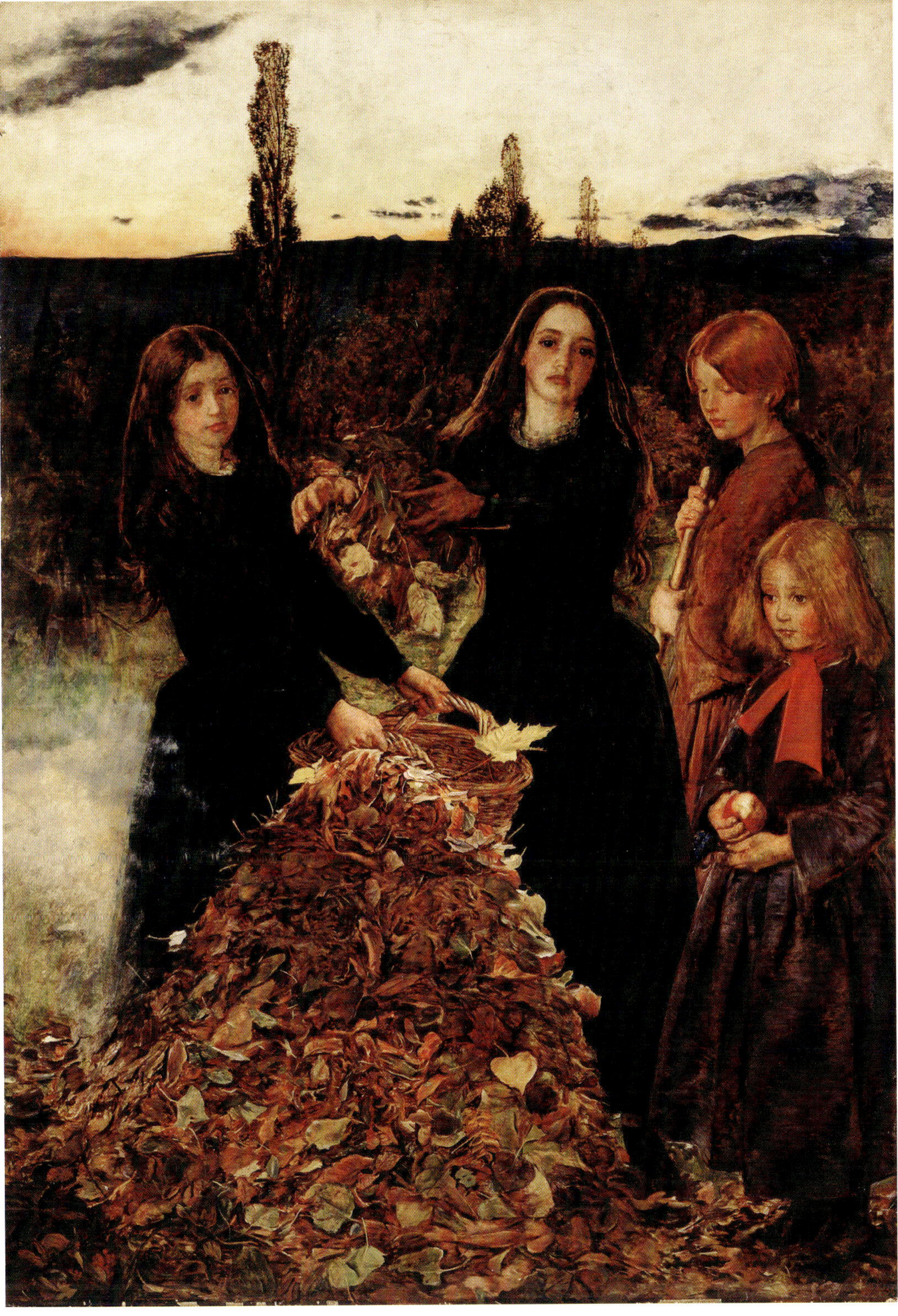

Fig. 24. John Everett Millais, *Autumn Leaves*, 1855–56. Oil on canvas, 41 x 29⅛ in. (104.3 x 74 cm). Manchester Art Gallery

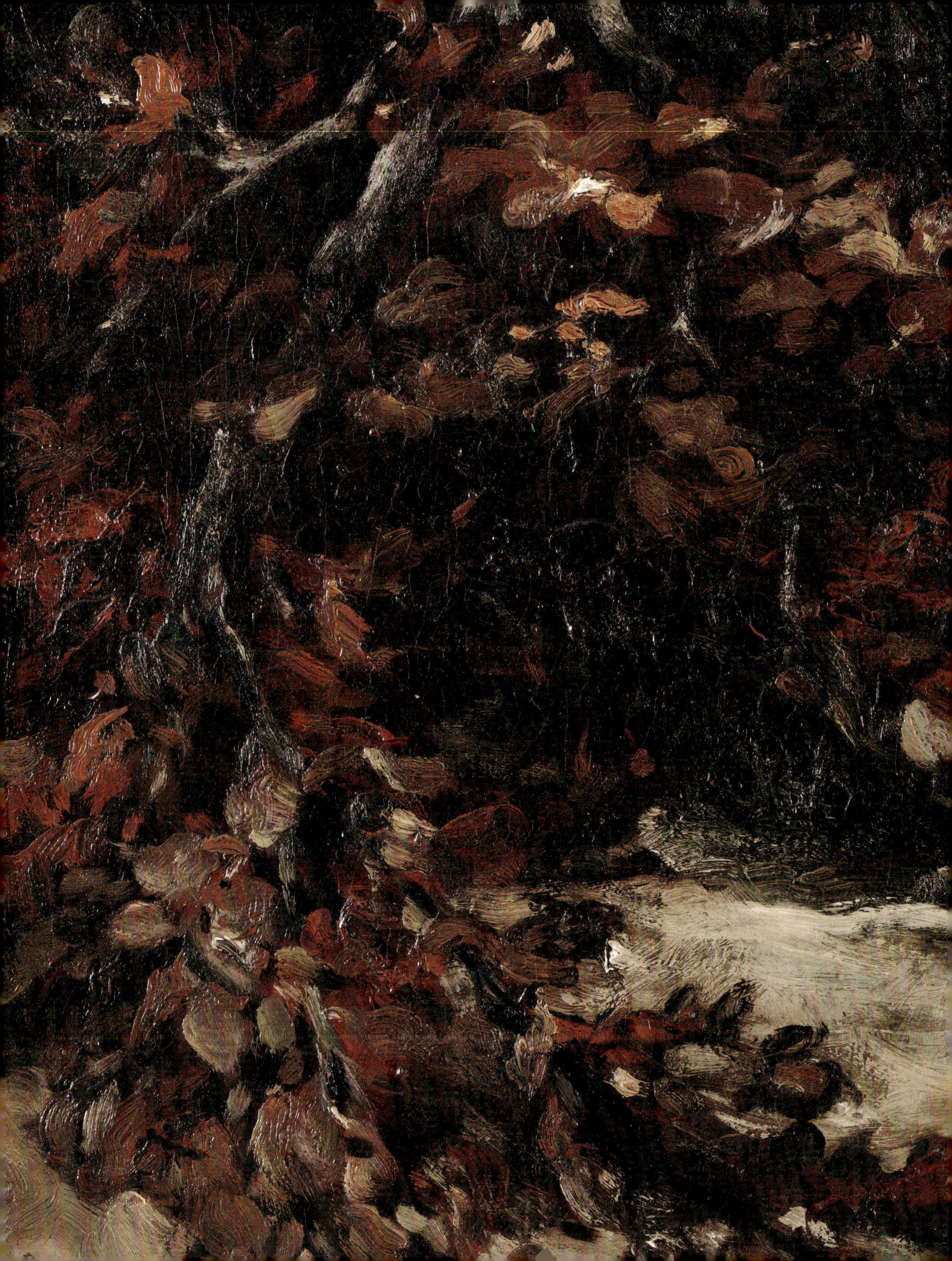

upon the great tradition of English child portraiture but also upon a recent masterpiece by the most exciting and influential English artist of his own generation.[51]

The association of youth with transience and the image of fallen leaves recur in the work of Tennyson and many other Victorian poets, major and minor. Among them was none other than Fanny Kemble, May's famous aunt and at this time Leighton's regular transatlantic correspondent. As a writer Kemble was to be known mainly for autobiographical works, especially her antislavery *Journal of a Residence on a Georgian Plantation in 1838–1839* (1863), but she also published plays and some poetry. This "Song," taken from the collection of her poems published in Boston in 1859, well represents the strain of melancholy that runs through her poetic works:

I sing the yellow leaf,
That rustling strews
The wintry path, where grief
Delights to muse,
Spring's early violet, that sweetly opes
Its fragrant leaves to the young morning's kiss,
Type of our youth's fond dreams, and cherished hope,
Will soon be this:
A sere and yellow leaf,
That rustling strews
The wintry path, where grief
Delights to muse.
The summer's rose, in whose rich hues we read
Pleasure's gay bloom, and love's enchanting bliss,
And glory's laurel, waving o'er the dead,
Will soon be this:
A sere and yellow leaf,
That rustling strews
The wintry path, where grief
Delights to muse.[52]

Fig. 25. Frederic Leighton, *May Sartoris*, detail (see fig. 19)

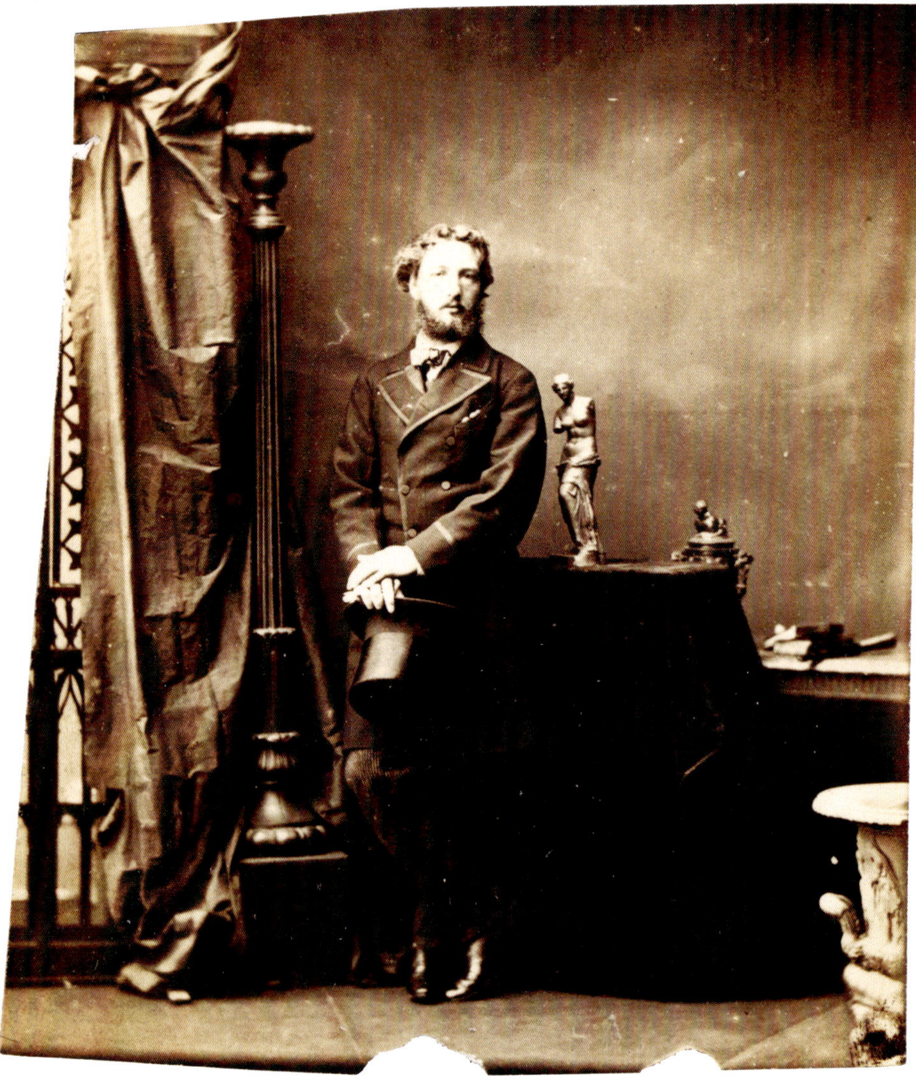

Fig. 26. Frederic Leighton, early 1860s. Photograph by Camille Silvy. Victoria and Albert Museum, London

Leighton did not set his portrait of May among the dead leaves of autumn or winter. The general state of the vegetation and the wheat sheaves in the background suggest late summer. But he introduced some of the same feeling, a sense of youth attended by mortality—the age-old imagery of Death and the Maiden—in the form of the felled beech tree that is such an unexpectedly insistent presence behind his sitter. There were felled trees to be seen at Westbury; the cutting of timber was a major source of income for the estate.[53] It is possible that the portrait refers to some incident involving May in a riding habit near such a tree. Many portraits must contain references to family stories now difficult or impossible to reclaim, although May's action and demeanor seem neither particular enough for an anecdote nor humorous enough for an in-joke. Even if locality and anecdote did provide starting points in the conception of the portrait, however, Leighton was the kind of artist who would have had higher aspirations in mind, aiming to create not merely a portrait but a resonant work of art. He shared in the growing tendency of nineteenth-century portraitists, especially those who were not portrait specialists, to take portraiture beyond the description of an individual person and into universal realms of meaning. His motive in affording the felled tree such prominence was to set a certain poetic tone. Like the ruin in the background, a more conventional symbol of the idea that all things must pass, it is an image of transience and loss.

We can be sure that Leighton and Adelaide, as friends in art, discussed May's portrait thoroughly—and that if its mood is somber, then such a mood must have been what, together, they intended. Melancholy intimations may have been a commonplace of Victorian art and literature, but what would lead this artist and this patron in such a direction as they planned this portrait? It had little to do with May or Leighton, one suspects, but much to do with Adelaide and the sense of loss that pervaded her outlook on life. The prospect of celebrating the daughter's beauty could not but have kindled some feelings of regret in the portly mother, reflections on how she too had once been young and attractive, her usual sense that life had been a disappointment. Even beyond this, though, Adelaide had reason to be mournful. She was only in her mid-forties, but she and her sister had already lost their parents and two brothers. Both brothers had died in 1857. The elder, John—Thackeray's friend and a distinguished philologist—succumbed to pneumonia. The younger, Henry, who was Adelaide's favorite, died insane after several years in an asylum. Soon—on June 29, 1861—would come the first death among the beloved friends of her Roman circle, that of Elizabeth Barrett Browning.[54]

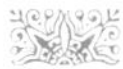

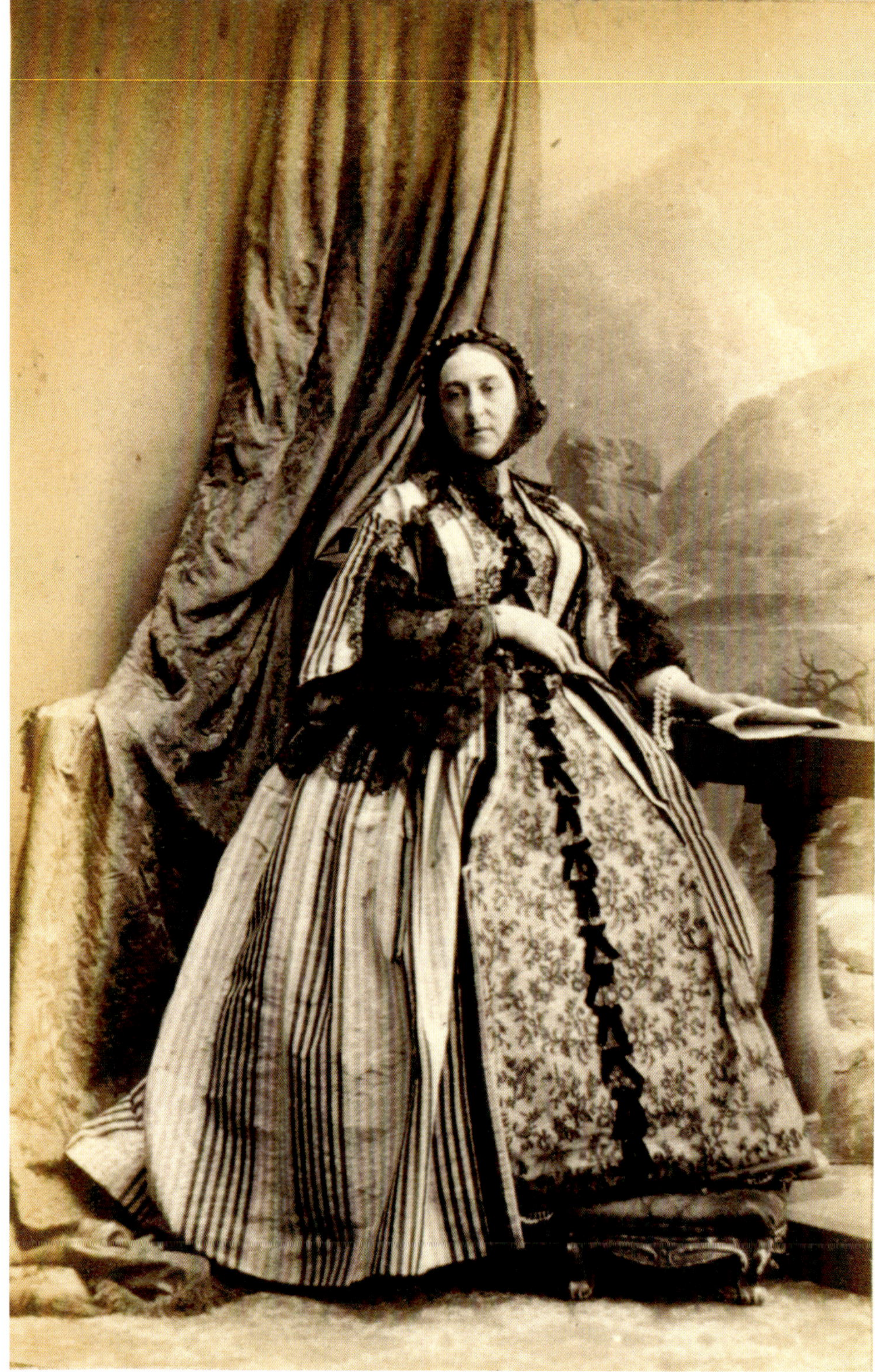

Fig. 27. Adelaide Sartoris, 1860. Photograph by Camille Silvy. National Portrait Gallery, London

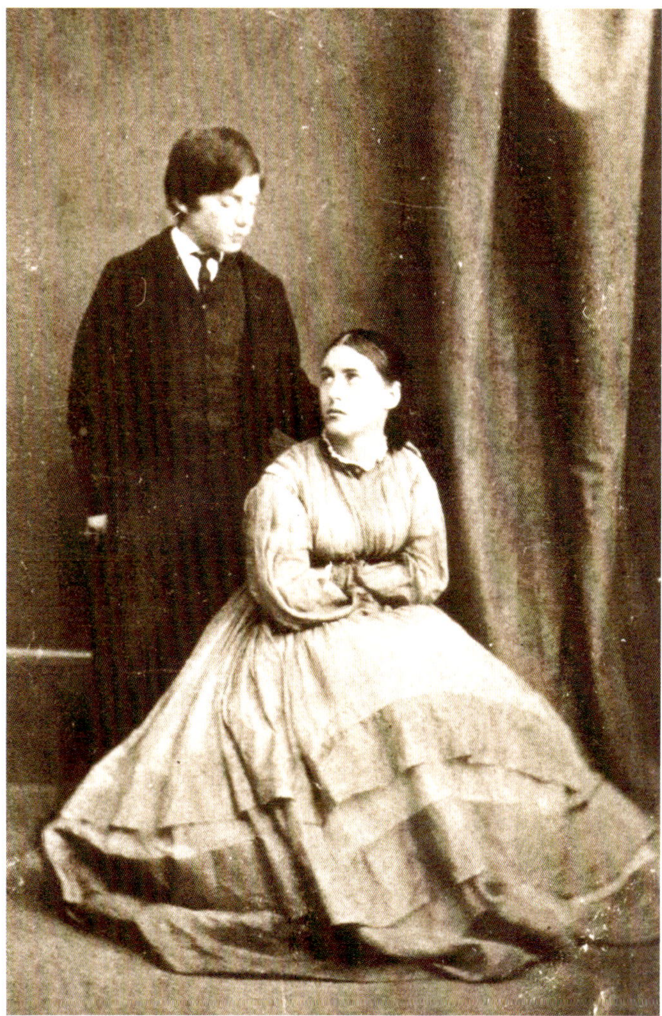

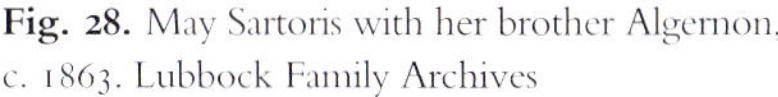

Fig. 28. May Sartoris with her brother Algernon, c. 1863. Lubbock Family Archives

IN 1863, ON THE DEATH OF HIS RICH UNCLE EDWARD TUNNO, EDWARD SARTORIS INHERITED the Tunno fortune along with the estate of Warnford Park, and this would be the Sartorises' next home.[55] By the following year they were also keeping a fashionable London residence at 9 Park Place, off St. James's. May began to take part in the round of parties, often musical, that was their social life in town. Her mother's daughter, she had a fine voice and sang arias from Verdi.[56] Leighton made a comic drawing of her with Adelaide and himself in a party incident that is hard to fathom but which certainly involved an explosion (fig. 29). The accompanying lines parody the old rhyme about Guy Fawkes's conspiracy to blow up the Houses of Parliament, "Remember, remember, the fifth of November."

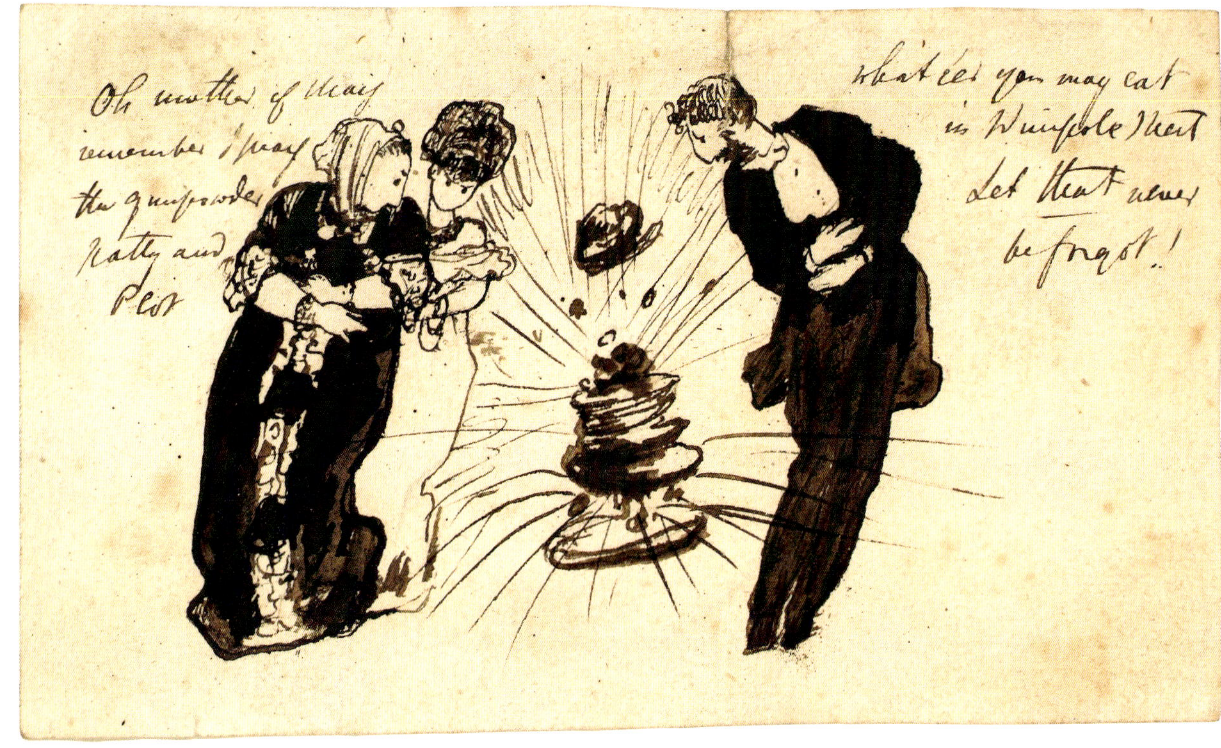

Fig. 29. Frederic Leighton, *Oh mother of May . . . , etc.*, c. 1865. Pen and ink, 3¼ x 5½ in. (13.9 x 8.1 cm). Leighton House Museum, London

Adelaide flourished as a hostess in London as she had in Rome and Paris. Thackeray's daughter remembered her at Park Place in a velvet brocaded dress, looking like a painting by Tintoretto, and nostalgic as ever: "I have everything a woman could wish for, my friends and my home, my husband and my children, and yet sometimes a wild longing comes over me to be back, if only for an hour, on the stage again, and living once more as I did in those adventurous times."[57] When at Warnford, May and her mother devoted time and energy to helping run a school for poor children.[58] There were frequent house parties, and Leighton was, of course, a regular. Whether Adelaide hung the completed portrait of May at Warnford or at Park Place is unknown but, given its background of Hampshire hillsides, she may have felt it would be more at home in the country.

It was at Warnford that Adelaide took to writing fiction. The main inspiration for her most successful work as an author, *A Week in a French Country-House*, was a house party given by her sister-in-law, the marquise de l'Aigle, in the fall of 1863. The marquise lived in the grand Château du Francport, north of Paris in the forest of Compiègne. Adelaide based the story on memories of the idyllic time she spent there combined with observations of her own house parties. It was published first in installments in the February, March, and April 1867 issues of the *Cornhill Magazine*, then as a separate volume. The story is a *roman à clef* featuring pen portraits of the author's artistic and cosmopolitan set: the character of Ursula Hamilton is based on her sister Fanny, and that of Monsieur Kiowski, an impulsive, beauty-loving artist gifted in music and languages, on Leighton. It appeared with two illustrations by Leighton himself. "Drifting" (fig. 30), which shows the party in a boat on the river, includes his self-portrait as Kiowski (far right, tending the rudder) and an idealized portrait of Adelaide as the hostess of the party, the widowed Madame Olympe, comtesse de Caradec (second from the right, singing). Her hair is dressed much as in Leighton's drawing of Adelaide in Paris. The model for Madame Olympe's sixteen-year-old daughter Jeanne, shown with an oar across her lap, could well have been May, and that for Madame Olympe's

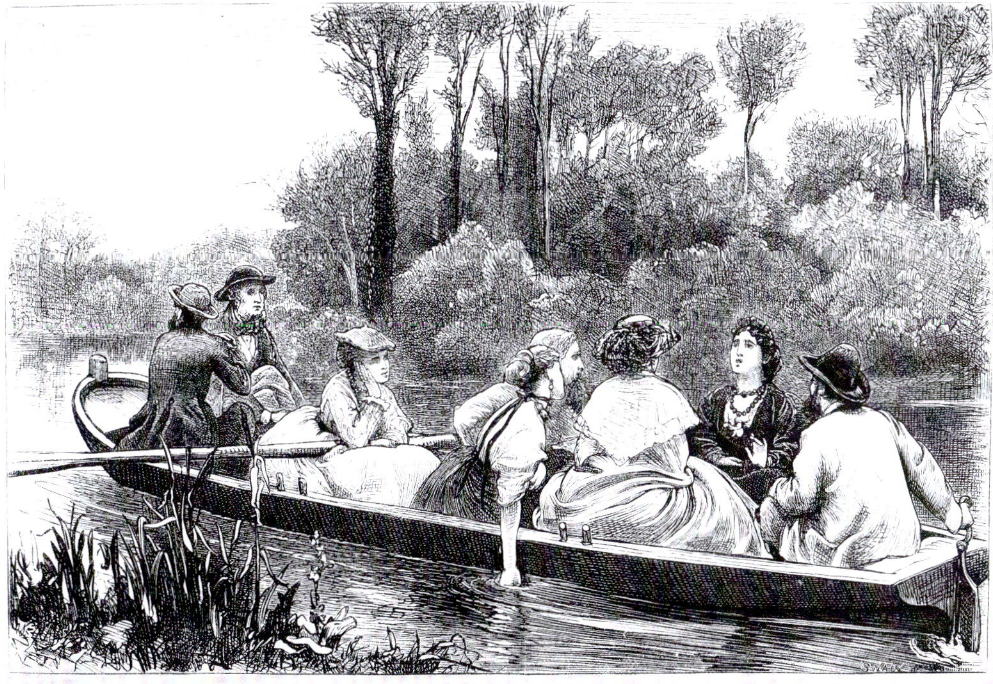
DRIFTING.

Fig. 30. Frederic Leighton, "Drifting," illustration to Adelaide Sartoris, *A Week in a French Country-House*, wood-engraving by Joseph Swain, London, 1867

brother, Monsieur Charles, the man with sideburns seated at the prow, could perhaps have been Edward Sartoris.[59]

Adelaide's description of this river outing reveals an undeniable preciousness, both on her own part as an author and on the part of her *alter ego* in the story, Madame Olympe. But it is effective all the same, and shows sensitivities that had surely played into her discussions with Leighton as to the look and feel of her daughter's portrait—an eye for colors in nature and a keen melancholy about the passage of time and the cycles of life:

> What an evening it was! One whole side of the heavens was of a deep solemn rose-colour, with a wondrous diaper of red brown leaves embroidered upon it by the branches of a screen of trees which stood out in strong relief against it: the other side was a blaze of golden fire. This effect lasted the longest: it only seemed to grow into an ever-deepening amber, haunting that half of heaven like some brooding passionate regret, while the rose hue passed first into violet, then into dark purple, and then faded away into still silver grey. Soft opal tints came down from the skies and lay upon the face of the waters, as we rowed away from all the glory into a world of delicate twilight shadow. Suddenly, from the grey bank, burned out a single orange-coloured leaf. Oh! Who shall explain the strange mystery by which one feels stabbed to the heart with a sharp pang of delight at some unexpected apparition of this kind? We all called aloud in one unanimous voice of salutation, as we floated past the little lonely flame. Presently the surface of the river became black as liquid ebony, the moon got up, and a pleasant rhythm of plashing oars, always accompanied by a bright flash of light, was all that marked our gentle progress through the water.
>
> "Ah! Will no one sing and make this quite, quite perfect?" said Madame Olympe.
>
> Monsieur Kiowski began the well-known air of the Sorrento boatmen, the *Fata d'Amalfi*, and Ursula joined in a second. While they sang, Jeanne and René pulled in their oars, and we went drifting—drifting—drifting along in soft darkness, listening to the passionate southern sounds. I could not help thinking that, perhaps when I am dying, that solitary leaf will burn into my heart once more, as I drift silently with closed eyes into the waters of the other life.[60]

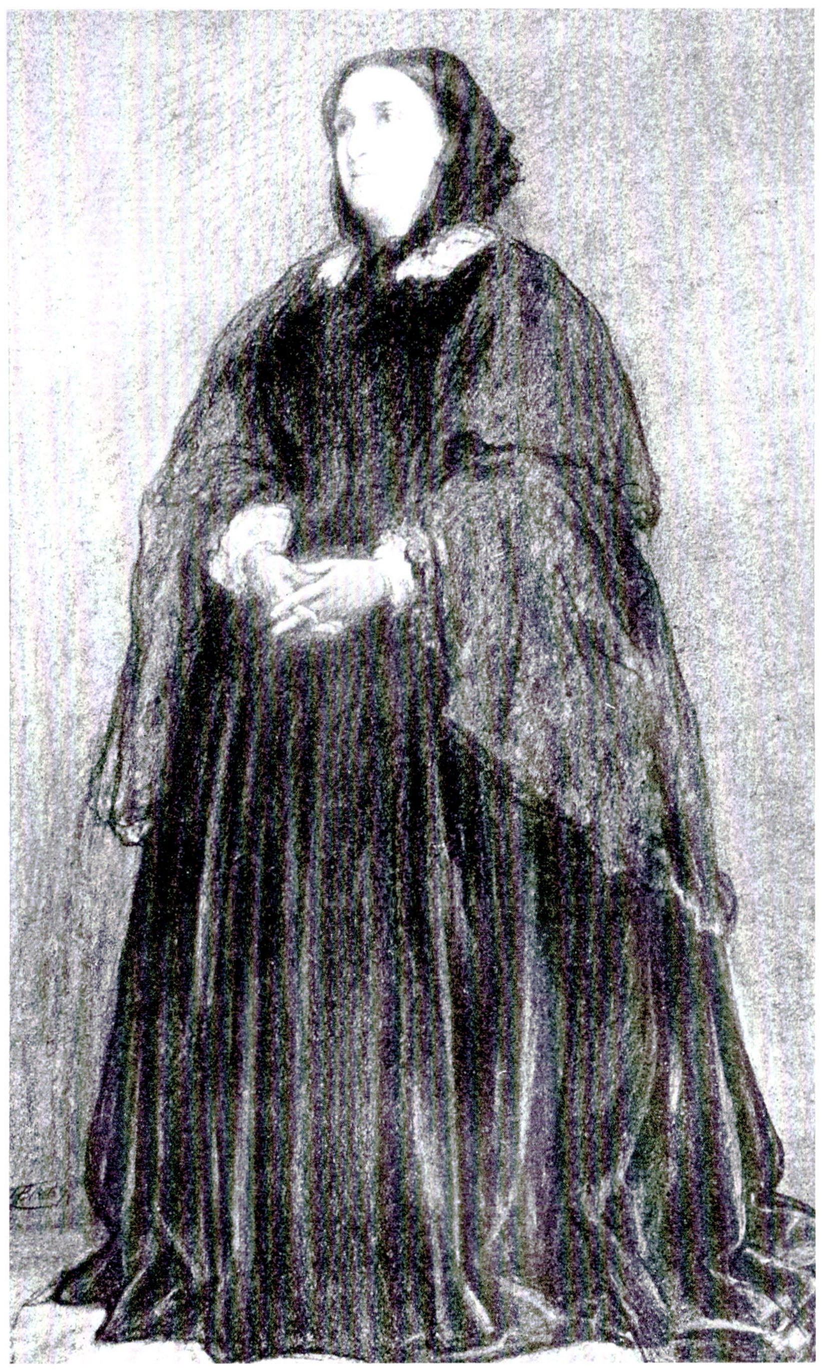

Fig. 31. Frederic Leighton, *Adelaide Sartoris*, 1867. Chalk drawing, made for Adelaide's friend Georgiana, Lady Bloomfield. Present whereabouts unknown. Reproduced from Mrs. Russell Barrington, *The Life, Letters and Work of Frederic Leighton*, London, 1906

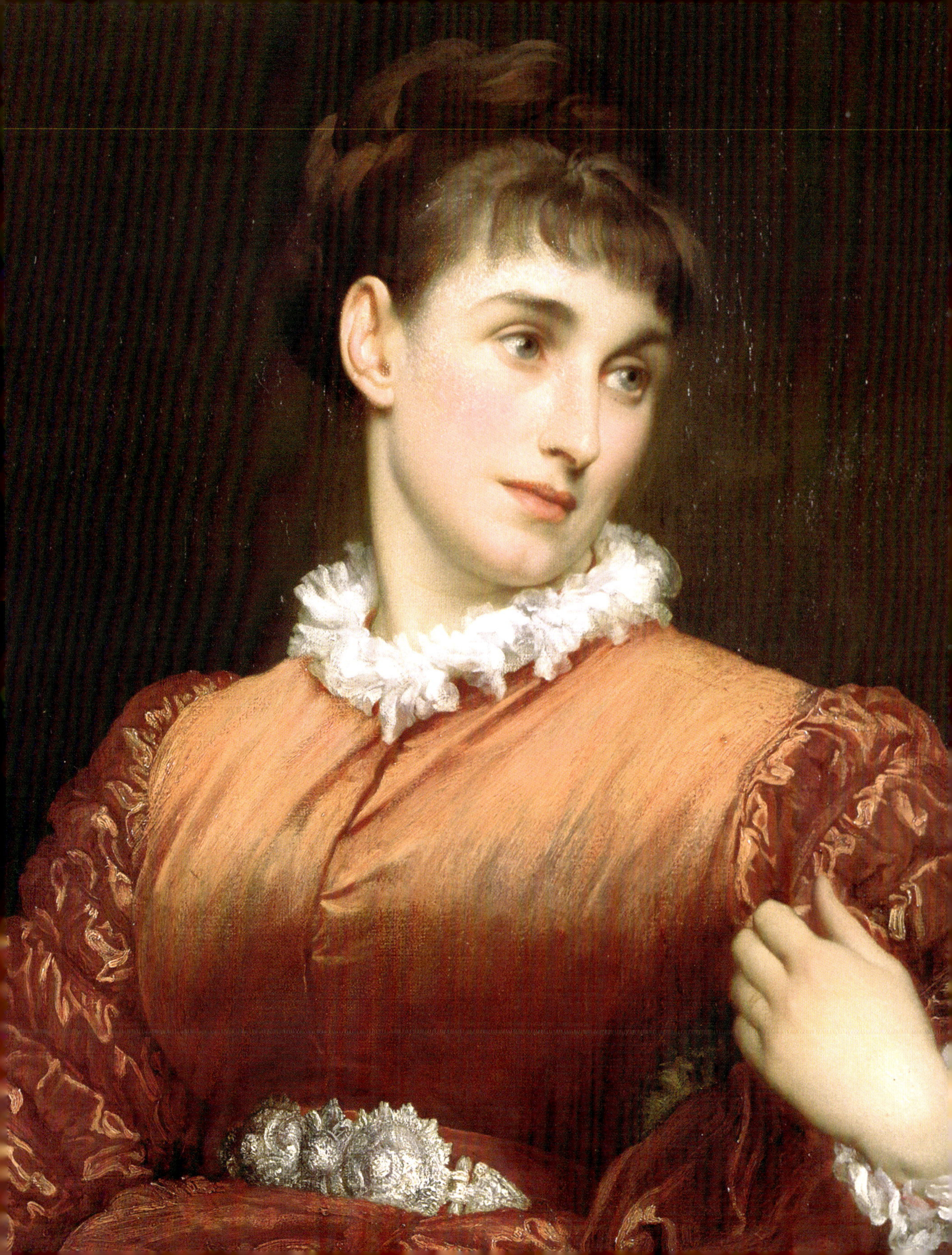

Later Lives

May Sartoris was still unmarried and living at home, and it must surely have occurred to her, to her parents, and to Leighton himself that he might become her suitor. He was doing well in his career, and in 1866 he moved into an impressive new house and studio in Holland Park Road, Kensington (now the Leighton House Museum). The age difference between him and May was an acceptable fifteen years, about the same as that between him and Adelaide in the other direction. At the time of the move he was thirty-five and May was twenty or twenty-one. If anything were ever to happen, the time was surely ripe; but nothing did, and Leighton would remain a lifelong bachelor.

In 1868 the Sartoris family also moved again, leaving Warnford for another grand country residence in Hampshire, Warsash House (see fig. 16). It was a mansion in a large park, with gardens sloping down to the Hamble River, which flows into Southampton Water and the Solent. This was to be Adelaide and Edward's home for the rest of their lives. They made extensive improvements to the house in an Italianate style and continued to live well and entertain frequently, keeping a household of a dozen servants.[61] From 1868 to 1874 Edward sat as Member of Parliament for Carmarthenshire in south Wales, where he also owned the estate of Llangennech Park. He was a Liberal, voting with the Gladstone government of those years. Meanwhile, as ever, Adelaide saw a great deal of Leighton. In August 1869

Fig. 32. Frederic Leighton, *May Evans Gordon*, detail (see fig. 36)

they went together to the French resort of Vichy, her doctor having advised her to take a spa cure. Every year she was becoming more obese, more a prey to ill health, and Leighton took on the role of nurse as well as traveling companion. "He is an angel and no mistake," Adelaide wrote to May while on a later trip through Italy. "Neither one's father—nor one's mother—and certainly not one's husband or one's brother could take half the tender care of one that he does of me."[62]

May was to make a less prestigious match than Leighton would have been, but one that brought her happiness. On April 19, 1871, she married Henry Evans Gordon, a stockbroker. He was the son of Major-General Charles Evans Gordon, governor of the Royal Military Hospital at Netley. Since Netley is on Southampton Water near Warsash, presumably the couple met through some local connection. The wedding took place at Warsash village church. The smaller portrait of May that Leighton made about this time is as sensuous a piece of painting as any in his life as an artist (fig. 33). He shows her wearing a veil, and the work may indeed have been a wedding gift to the couple.[63] After a honeymoon in Scotland, May and Henry returned to live at Warsash Lodge, a considerable house standing in its own grounds on the Warsash estate.[64] But by 1872 they had moved to the village of Ightham in Kent, where Henry's family had ties. Their new, more modest home was called Prestons.[65] It would remain their country residence for the rest of their lives, although they would also have homes in London and spend much of their time there, at least as long as Henry was working in the City.[66]

In 1873 the family was devastated by the death of May's elder brother, Greville, in a riding accident. He was thirty and pursuing a career in the diplomatic service. Adelaide was deeply distraught and never recovered. A few grief-stricken years later her health became worse than ever. She went into a steep decline, becoming weak and emaciated from the effects of diabetes, and died, at home at Warsash, on August 6, 1879. She was sixty-four. The funeral took place at the church of St. Peter's in Ightham. Greville had been buried in the churchyard there, and Adelaide was buried with him. Her chief mourners were Edward, May and Henry, her younger son Algernon and his wife Nellie, Leighton, and her friend Anne Procter, whom she had known since childhood.[67] In the following year May edited a posthumous volume of Adelaide's stories under the title *Past Hours*. In the preface she paid

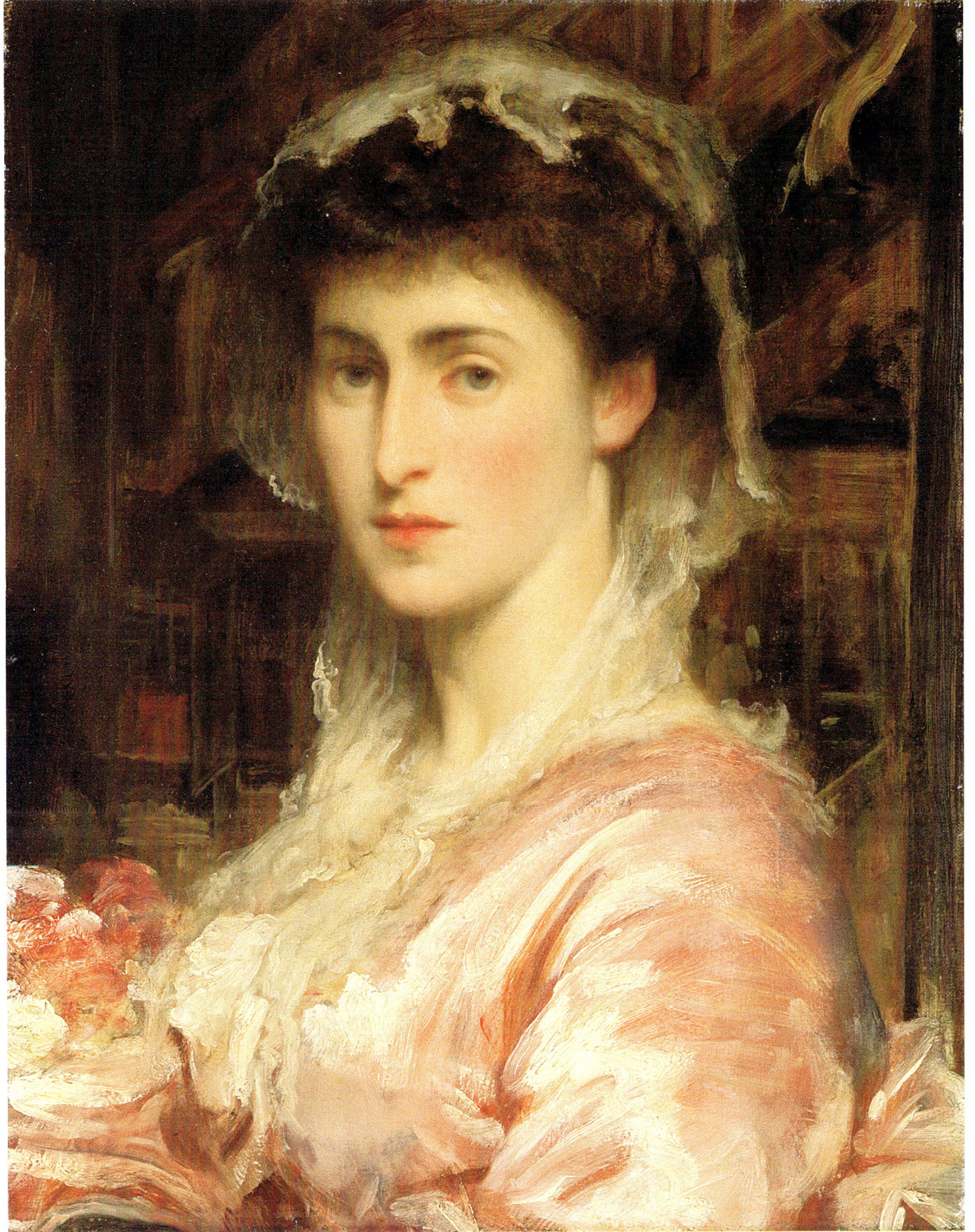

Fig. 33. Frederic Leighton, *May Sartoris*, c. 1871. Oil on canvas, 21 x 17 in. (53.3 x 43.1 cm). Private collection

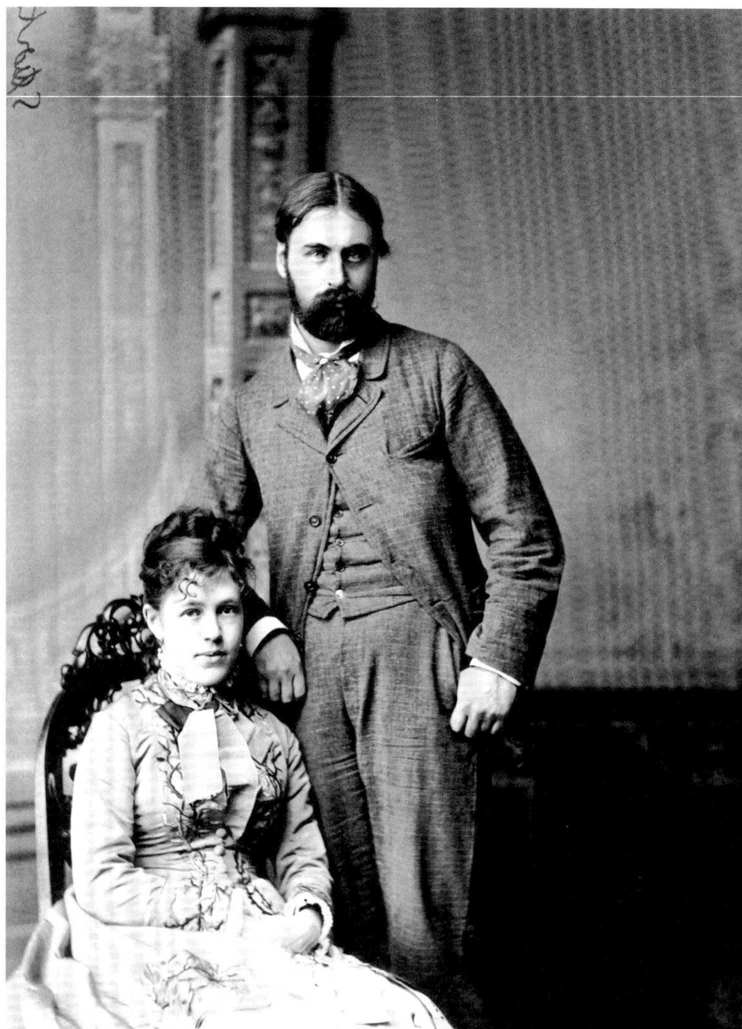

Fig. 34. Algernon Sartoris and Nellie Grant, 1874. Library of Congress, Washington, D.C.

tribute to her mother as "one whose large sympathies and greatness of soul never failed to attract and bring out all that was best and most noble in every one who approached her."[68]

May's surviving brother Algernon (known as Algy), the apple-cheeked boy whom Leighton painted in Rome, brought the family almost as much distress in his life as Greville in his death. As an army officer assigned to the British legation in Washington, he met and courted Nellie Grant, daughter of President Ulysses S. Grant (fig. 34). With the reluctant consent of the president, they were married on May 21, 1874, in a grand wedding at the White House. Adelaide was too upset over Greville to attend. Algy and Nellie came to live in England and had four children, although the marriage was never happy. Leighton seems to have kept up with them, as with all the Sartoris family, and in 1881 showed a portrait of Nellie, unfortunately now lost, at the Grosvenor Gallery exhibition in London. The problem was that Algy was a bad lot. He was a heavy drinker, probably adulterous, and widely disliked, nowhere more than in the United States. He died of pneumonia at Capri in 1893, aged only forty-one, and Nellie returned home.[69] May and Henry seem, at least at times, to have provided a London home for Algy and Nellie's two daughters, Rosemary and Vivien.[70]

Unlike her mother and her brothers, May lived a long and satisfying life. She and Henry had four children, all girls: Catherine Hermione, Jean Adelaide, Margaret Evelyn, and Mary Frances. The middle names of Jean and Mary were, of course, tributes to May's mother and aunt. She and Leighton remained close until his death. He was like an uncle to the children, and it became a family tradition for him to treat them to a box at the pantomime every New Year's Day.[71] In 1875 he made his last portrait of her, completing a trio of likenesses that followed her from girlhood to young womanhood to motherhood (figs. 35, 36); this was the year in which her third daughter, Margaret, was born. Again, there is an air of fancy dress about May's clothing—this time historical, gently likening her to a noblewoman of the Renaissance. The perky little dog—which, like May, responds to an unseen someone to the right—calls to mind the dogs in Titian's famous paintings of reclining Venuses.

May lived comfortably with Henry—whom Leighton also painted (fig. 38)—but they were never to be as wealthy as May's parents. When her father died in 1888 he left them Warsash Lodge, the house in which they had lived when they were first married, but the chief beneficiary of the estate was Algy, the wayward brother.[72] May kept up her singing as a member of the Bach Choir and her liking for theater as a talented amateur actress, and passed her enthusiasms on to her daughters. "With their love of art and music, and their delight in amateur theatricals," a granddaughter later recalled, they were a "gentle, deeply affectionate family circle."[73] May seems never to have yearned for the professional stage and found an identity in wifehood, motherhood, eventually grandmotherhood, that was free of the nagging regret suffered by her own mother. She had a good sense of humor. Her nickname in the family was "Marmee," a reference to Alma "Marmee" March, the mother of four

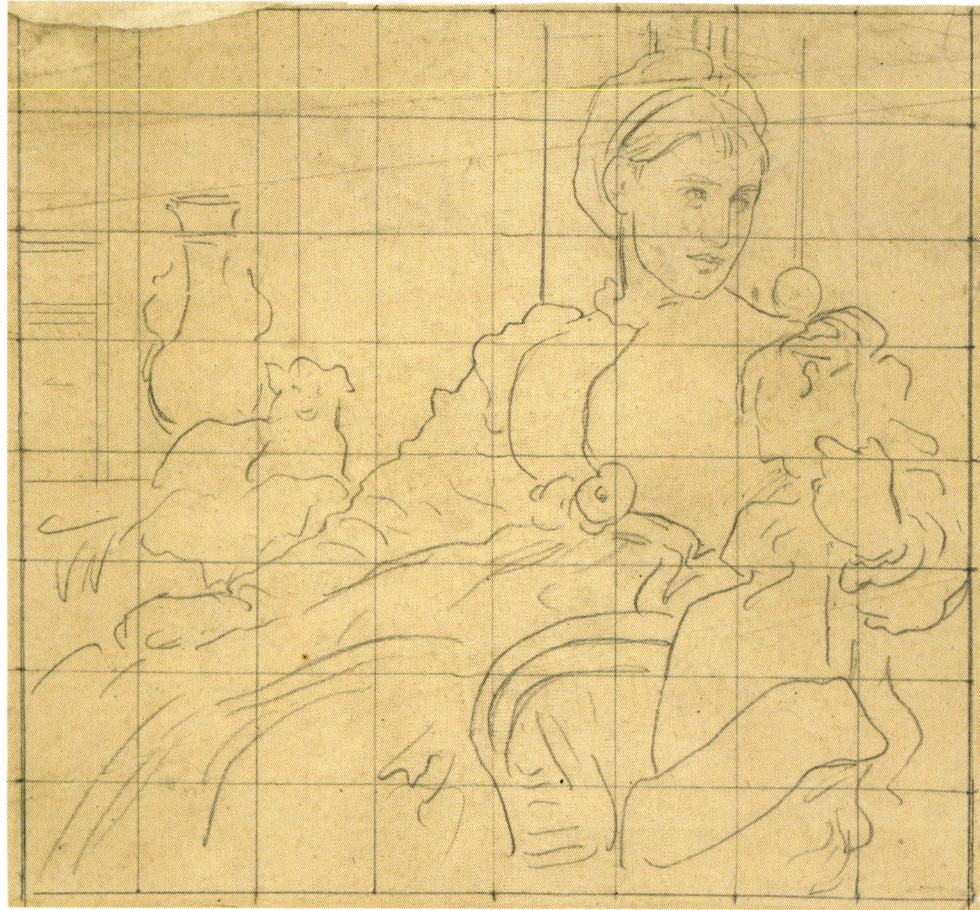

Fig. 35. Frederic Leighton, Sketch for *May Evans Gordon*, 1875. Pencil on tracing paper, 8⅝ x 9⅜ in. (21.9 x 23.9 cm), squared-up for transfer to canvas. Royal Academy of Arts, London.

daughters in Louisa May Alcott's *Little Women* (1868). For reasons unknown, Henry was called "Pino," which in Italy is usually the nickname for a Giuseppe. A friend described him as "perhaps the most clever and lovable man I have ever met . . . a fine raconteur, accomplished in music and in painting, and an interesting political thinker."[74]

Meanwhile Leighton had become one of the senior statesmen of British art. In 1878 he fulfilled Thackeray's long-ago prediction by being elected president of the Royal Academy, the highest post in the profession. He carried out his presidential duties with polish, moving easily in high society, and encouraged the efforts of young and innovative fellow artists. In the most ambitious of his own works he continued with friezelike figure compositions, and the monumental *Captive Andromache* stands as his masterpiece (fig. 37). The craving for physical beauty that gave rise to such paintings is not always easy for viewers of today, with their

Fig. 36. Frederic Leighton, *May Evans Gordon*, 1875. Oil on canvas, 38½ x 40 in. (97.8 x 101.6 cm). Leighton House Museum, London

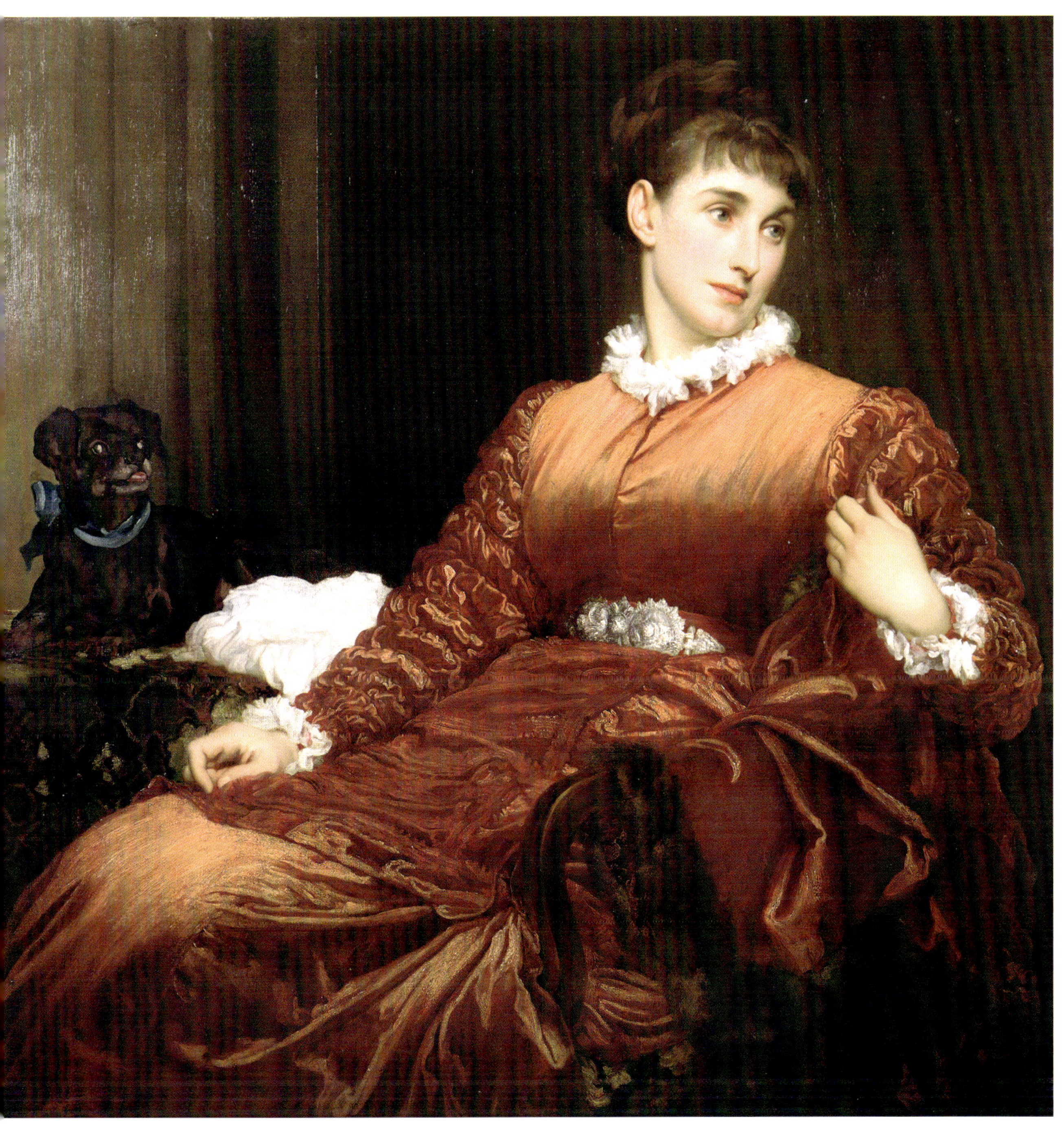

openness to the unbeautiful in art, even the anti-beautiful, to enter into. For Leighton and his friends in the Aesthetic Movement, the artist's calling was to cultivate beauty in his hothouse of a studio, to bring it back from the past, to save it from the ugliness and philistinism of the present. "Painting no longer the natural attaining of the sense of beauty & wonder that dwelt in all," he once jotted in a notebook. "The turmoil & complication of modern life make an artist's task incomparable [*sic*] more difficult and artificial but also enhances the value of the result."[75] He offered the people of industrial Britain an escape to ancient Greece as a world of Mediterranean beauty, health, abundance, and sunshine. His paintings were full of sensual and discreetly erotic delights. As with so much Victorian art, however, the prevailing mood was still melancholic. The joys of life were intensely felt, but typically bound up in nostalgia, yearning, or—as with the mournful, exiled Andromache—a tragic fate.

In the New Year Honours List of 1896, Leighton was created Baron Leighton of Stretton, becoming the first artist ever raised to the British peerage—since which time he has

Fig. 37. Frederic Leighton, *Captive Andromache*, c. 1887–88. Oil on canvas, 77½ x 160¼ in. (197 x 407 cm). Manchester Art Gallery

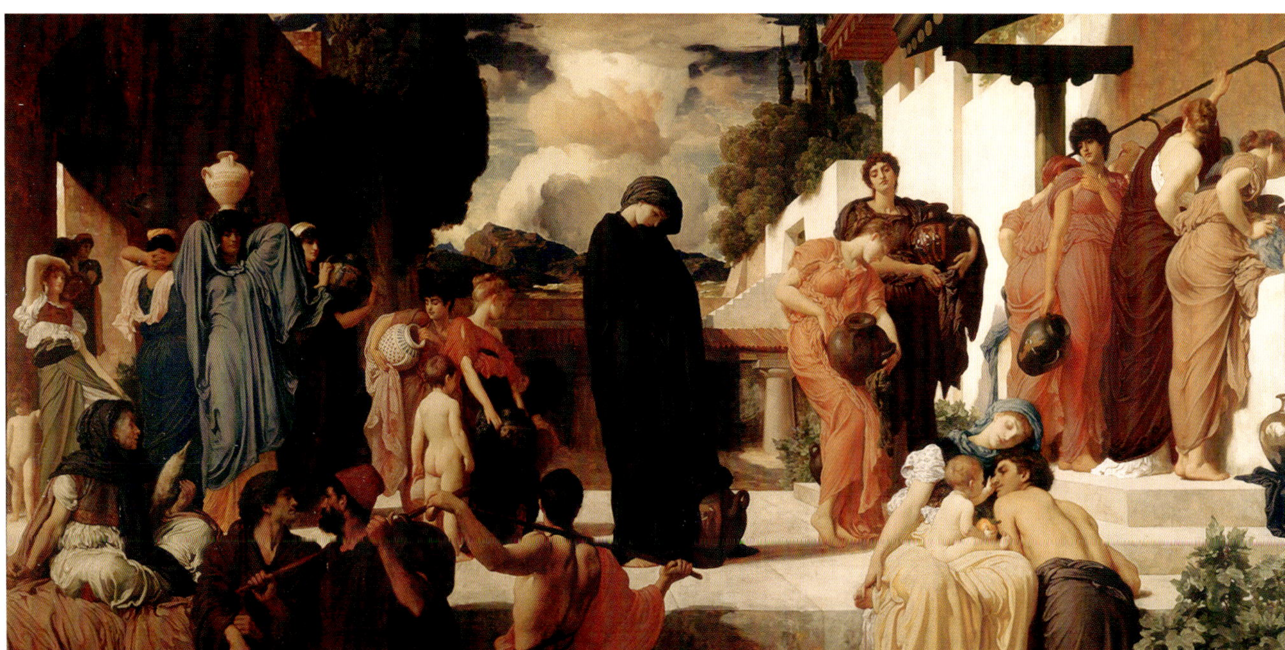

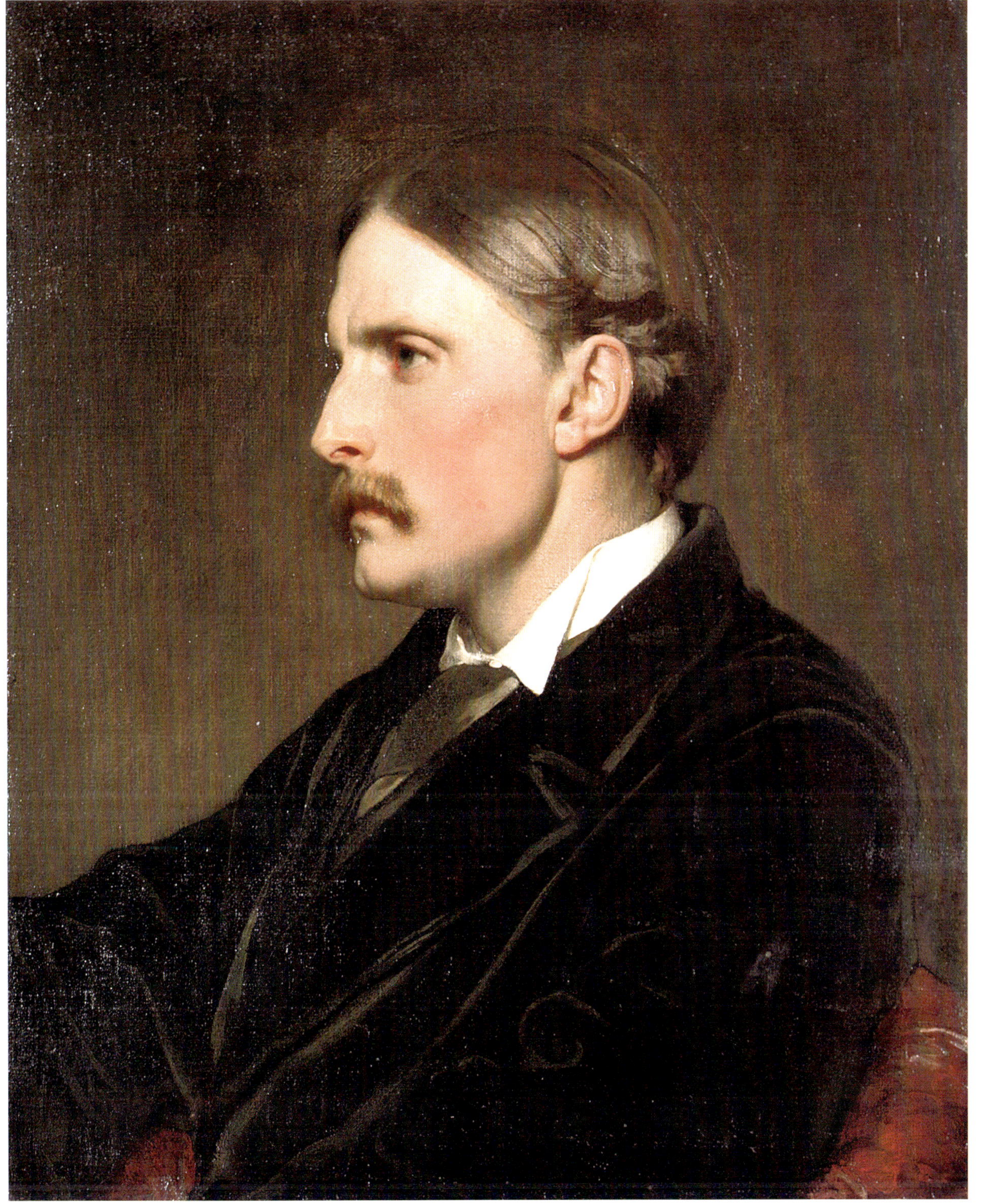

Fig. 38. Frederic Leighton, *Henry Evans Gordon*, 1876–77. Oil on canvas, 24 x 20 in. (61 x 50.8 cm). Private collection

commonly been referred to as Lord Leighton. He died just days later, on January 25, and was buried, amid much pomp, in St. Paul's Cathedral. Moved by the artist's death, the poet Algernon Charles Swinburne recalled meeting him and Adelaide on their visit to Vichy and wrote the elegy "An Evening at Vichy," in which he imagined him in heaven, hearing Adelaide sing again:

> The days that were outlighten the days that are,
> And eyes now darkened shine as the stars we see
> And hear not sing, impassionate star to star,
> As once we heard the music that haply he
> Hears, high in heaven if ever a voice may be
> The same in heaven, the same as on earth, afar
> From pain and earth as heaven from the heaving sea.
>
> A woman's voice, divine as a bird's by dawn
> Kindled and stirred to sunward, arose and held
> Our souls that heard, from earth as from sleep withdrawn,
> And filled with light as stars, and as stars compelled
> To move by might of music, elate while quelled,
> Subdued by rapture, lit as a mountain lawn
> By morning whence all heaven in the sunrise welled.
>
> And her the shadow of death as a robe clasped round
> Then: and as morning's music she passed away.
> And he then with us, warrior and wanderer, crowned
> With fame that shone from eastern on western day,
> More strong, more kind, than praise or than grief might say,
> Has passed now forth of shadow by sunlight bound,
> Of night shot through with light that is frail as May.[76]

When the Royal Academy honored Leighton with a commemorative exhibition in 1897, May and Henry lent a number of works in their possession, including the Kimbell portrait.

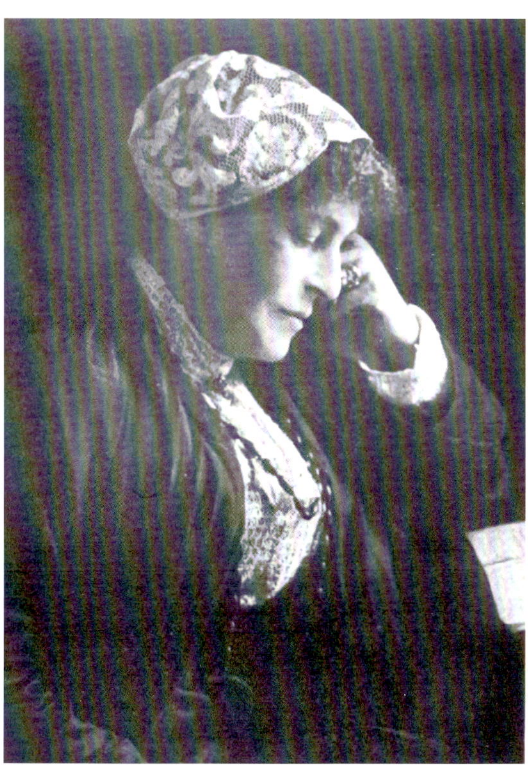

Fig. 39. May Evans Gordon, 1915. Lubbock Family Archives

It was the first time it had been displayed in public, some thirty-seven years after it was painted. By now May was in her fifties, with daughters reaching the age of marriageability. In 1899 her second daughter, Jean, married Lieutenant-General Sir William Thomas Furse, and in 1905 her third daughter, Margaret, married Sir Arthur Lyulph Stanley, later to become 5th Baron Stanley of Alderley. May must have been wounded by the death of her beloved Henry in 1909, aged only sixty-seven. But she seems to have spent her remaining years in quiet contentment at Ightham, where she lived with her unmarried daughters, Catherine and Mary. Looking more and more like her mother, she was "dearly beloved of all the village folk."[77] Margaret's daughter Adelaide Stanley remembered her with great affection:

> She was still beautiful in old age, with fine aquiline features and sad, deep-set eyes. She had an almost Rabelaisian sense of humour and, like my mother, was a brilliant mimic with an unerring eye for the ludicrous or pompous in character and situation. She was an excellent musician and linguist, a talented amateur painter with a gift for caricature and a writer of short stories and verse which, though they

are rather too sentimental in flavour for modern taste, nevertheless have a certain literary competence and period charm. Unlike my mother, she was a completely straightforward character, often surprisingly forceful in her opinions and judgements, and incapable of putting on an act or succumbing to self-pity. She was shy and reserved in the company of people she did not know well and sometimes would appear uncommunicative and aloof. But she had a deeply compassionate understanding of human nature and the gift of unlocking the heart of a child. She became the loved and loving companion and confidante of her headstrong and furiously self-willed little granddaughter.

After my grandfather died, she withdrew from the world and lived at Prestons with her two unmarried daughters, Clatten and Poppety (such were their nicknames), finding solace in gardening, painting, music and books. I remember her in a big cotton sunbonnet and galoshes, a trowel or fork in one hand and a wooden trug in the other, weeding, planting, staking, and pruning in her lovely flower garden with its sweeping view over the Kentish Weald. In the evenings she would play the piano or read to me or tell me stories, or teach me to play patience. She always wore a lace cap indoors and a black or lavender-grey silk dress with a lace fichu: and she chain-smoked, keeping the cigarette in her mouth and dropping the ash down the folds of the lace and silk.

I thought of Prestons as a haven from the hurly-burly of life at Alderley or Penrhos. It was a Victorian country house, gabled and tiled, of little architectural merit, but with a serene atmosphere. The interior was quite un-English, the panelled rooms being hung with Flemish tapestries and furnished with rather florid Italian pieces, carved, gilded and inlaid. Great china bowls filled with pot-pourri made every year by my grandmother scented the whole house. I remember nothing of nursery life or servants at Prestons—only my grandmother's presence and my love of being with her.[78]

Some of the elderly, chain-smoking May's sense of humor comes through in a letter she wrote during World War I to Margaret, who worried that she was in danger from Zeppelin raids: "Don't *fidget* about the Zeppelins . . . they really do not come our way and certainly would not waste bombs on Ightham."[79] She died on September 18, 1925, and was buried with her brother Greville, both her parents, and Henry, at St. Peter's, Ightham (fig. 40). A heart-shaped plaque on the grave bears her name with Henry's and the words "Herein is our love made perfect."

May passed on her theatrical genes to several of her descendants. Her daughter Margaret enthusiastically kept up the family tradition of theatricals and was an outstanding amateur actress.[80] Margaret's own daughters Adelaide and Pamela Stanley even went on to professional careers. Pamela played Ophelia in Leslie Howard's ill-fated Broadway production of *Hamlet* in 1936 and was celebrated for her performance as Queen Victoria in Laurence Housman's play *Victoria Regina,* which opened in London in 1937. Adelaide both acted and sang, and during World War II was a junior member of the group of entertainers known as the Crazy Gang. Another of May's grandchildren, Jean's daughter Judith Furse, was a character actress whose screen career spanned the 1930s to the 1970s. Often cast in overbearing, mannish roles, she was at her best as Sister Briony in the film *Black Narcissus* (1947). Judith's brother Roger Kemble Furse was a designer in film and theater who worked with Laurence Olivier and won Oscars for his work in both art direction and costume design on the Olivier film version of *Hamlet* (1948).

Fig. 40. Grave of members of the Sartoris and Evans Gordon families, Church of St. Peter's, Ightham

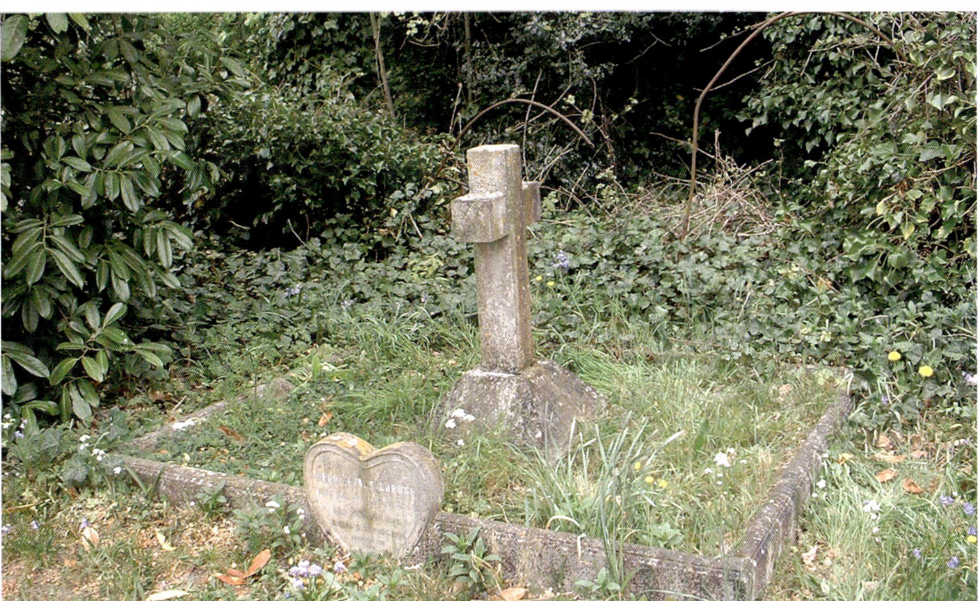

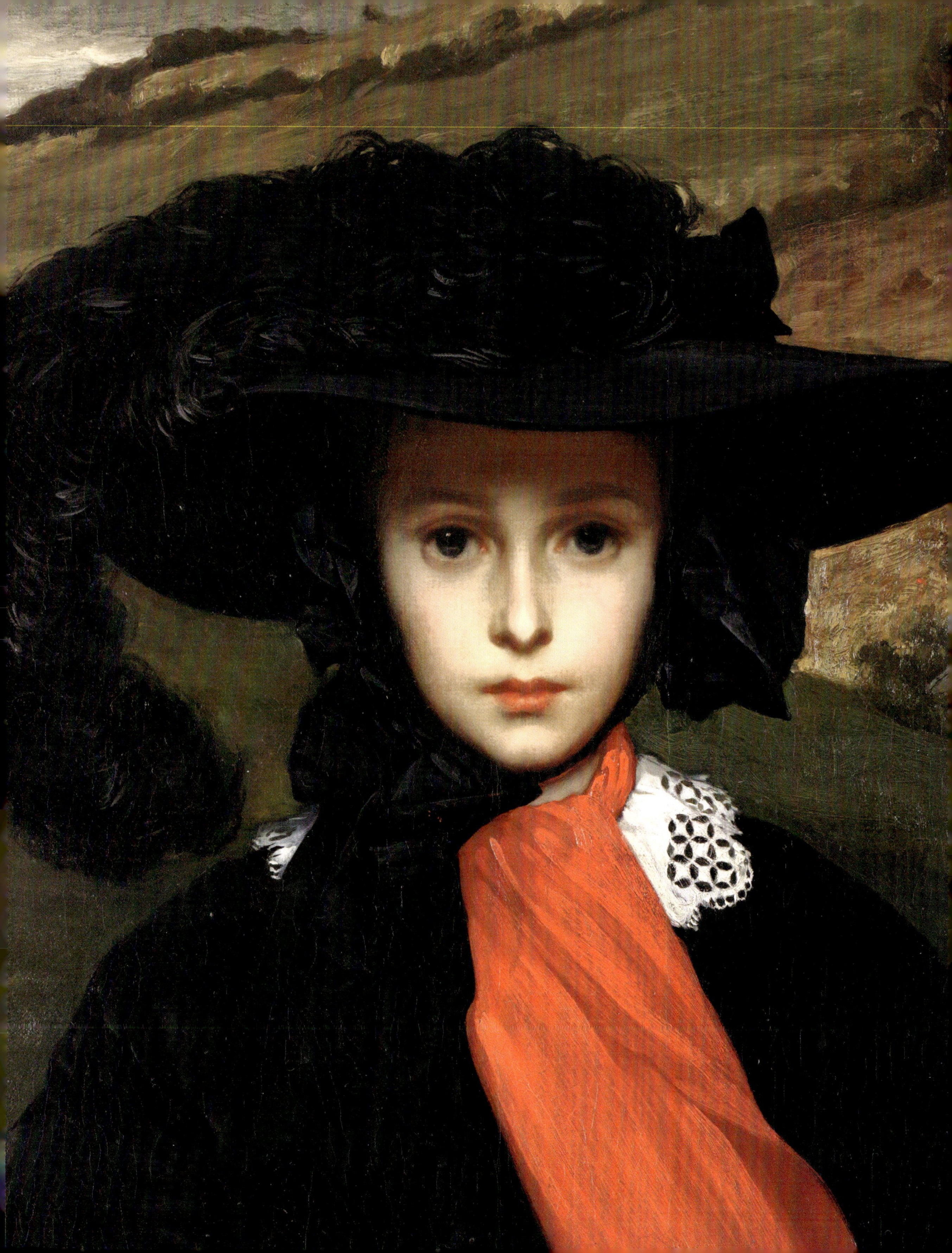

May in Texas

THE HISTORY OF THE OWNERSHIP OF MAY'S PORTRAIT IS DIFFICULT TO RECONSTRUCT in full. It might have passed to May and Henry at her father's death in 1888 or earlier than that, the only certainty being that it did belong to them by 1897. After May's own death in 1925 it appears to have passed to her daughter Margaret—now Lady Stanley—who lived at Alderley Park in Cheshire and Penrhos in Anglesey, north Wales. By the 1940s it was with Lady Stanley's daughter Adelaide, the actress and singer who had been so fond of May as a girl. Adelaide was married to the Hon. Maurice Fox Pitt Lubbock, son of Baron Avebury, and they lived in Lowndes Square, London.[81] The date and circumstances of the portrait's crossing the Atlantic are unknown, but by 1963 it was being offered for sale by Newhouse Galleries, New York. In their documentation of the work in a prospectus, Newhouse gave the previous owner as "Mrs. M. Turner, a relative of the sitter, London, England."[82] Nothing further is known of Mrs. Turner; if she was indeed related to May, it cannot have been closely. Newhouse had the portrait for only a short time before selling it to Kay Kimbell, founder of the Kimbell Art Museum.

The hugely successful Texas businessman Kay Kimbell had moved the headquarters of his Kimbell Milling Company to Fort Worth in 1924, building and operating grain elevators. Over the years he branched out into cottonseed oil presses and refineries, wholesale and retail food stores, railroads, oil, and insurance. He believed in diversification. Like many American

Fig. 41. Frederic Leighton, *May Sartoris*, detail (see fig. 19)

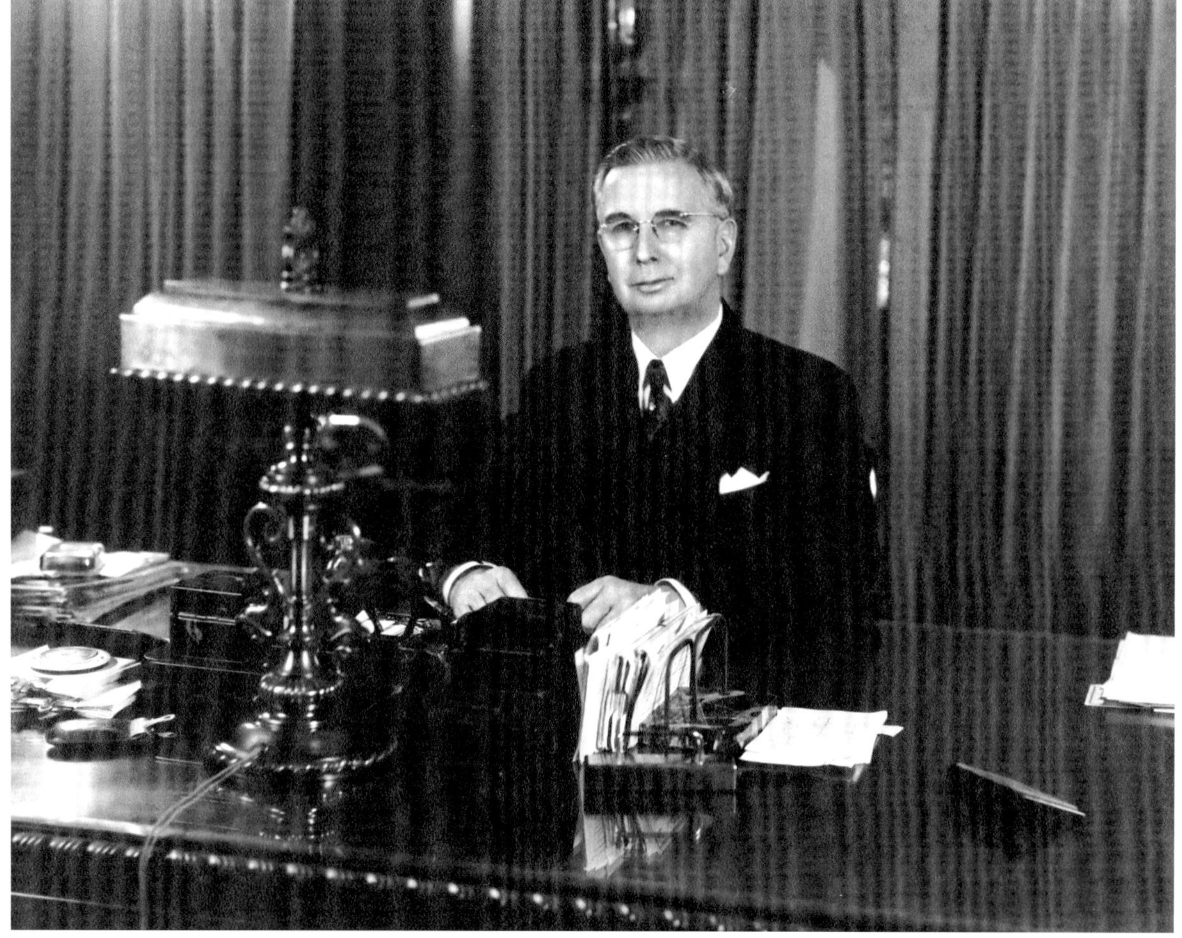

Fig. 42. Kay Kimbell, 1935

magnates of his time, he also took up art collecting, and the purchase of Leighton's portrait of May Sartoris is one of numerous instances in which he and his wife, Velma Kimbell, exercised their Anglophile taste.

Around 1900 there had begun a tremendous surge in the collecting of British art by wealthy Americans. The first decades of the twentieth century were the heyday of the great industrialist and financier collectors—notably Henry Clay Frick, J. Pierpont Morgan, Andrew W. Mellon, and Henry E. Huntington—and British portraiture was at least as important and desirable to them as any other field of old master painting. Not unlike

Leighton's paintings of ancient Greece in the nineteenth century, the works of Reynolds, Gainsborough, Lawrence, and other British portraitists offered such twentieth-century collectors a nostalgic refuge from the prosaic, workaday present, the dream of an idyllic, leisured, preindustrial society. The most dedicated Anglophile of them all was Huntington, the heart and soul of whose collection was a spectacular group of British portraits in full length. He formed the collection between 1911 and 1926, and the price he paid for Gainsborough's *Blue Boy* in 1921 (£182,200, then about $728,000) was a record for any painting of any national school.[83]

American Anglophile collecting dwindled in the Great Depression. Kay and Velma Kimbell came in at the tail end, but they pursued British art just as staunchly, if not generally at the same level of quality, as Huntington had. They began in 1935, when Velma took a liking to a painting by William Beechey of the artist's own children (fig. 43).[84] It was on show in an exhibition at the Carnegie Library in Fort Worth organized by the Ehrich-Newhouse Galleries of New York. She brought her husband to see the work, and he bought it from Bertram M. Newhouse, the then-partner of Walter Ehrich, on the exhibition's last day. It was the beginning of a long relationship between the Kimbells and Newhouse, who became for them what Joseph Duveen had been for the titanic American collectors of earlier times. During the first year after they met at the library, they bought at least eighteen paintings from him. He became their main source, educating them in art and searching out prospective acquisitions that suited their developing taste, as well as their distaste for high prices. They became close friends, and before long Kimbell had a financial stake in Newhouse's business.

In 1936, on the basis of their fledgling collection, the Kimbells, together with Kay's sister and brother-in-law, Dr. and Mrs. Coleman Carter, formed the Kimbell Art Foundation. It was from the Kimbell Art Foundation, incorporated under the laws of Texas for the purpose of founding and maintaining an art institute in Fort Worth, that the Kimbell Art Museum was to spring. The Kimbells would venture into other areas of art, but the dominant impetus in their collecting remained the taste for British portraiture. Almost incredibly, Kay Kimbell never went to England or anywhere else in Europe. But he did visit some of the great American collections, including Frick's in New York and Huntington's in San Marino,

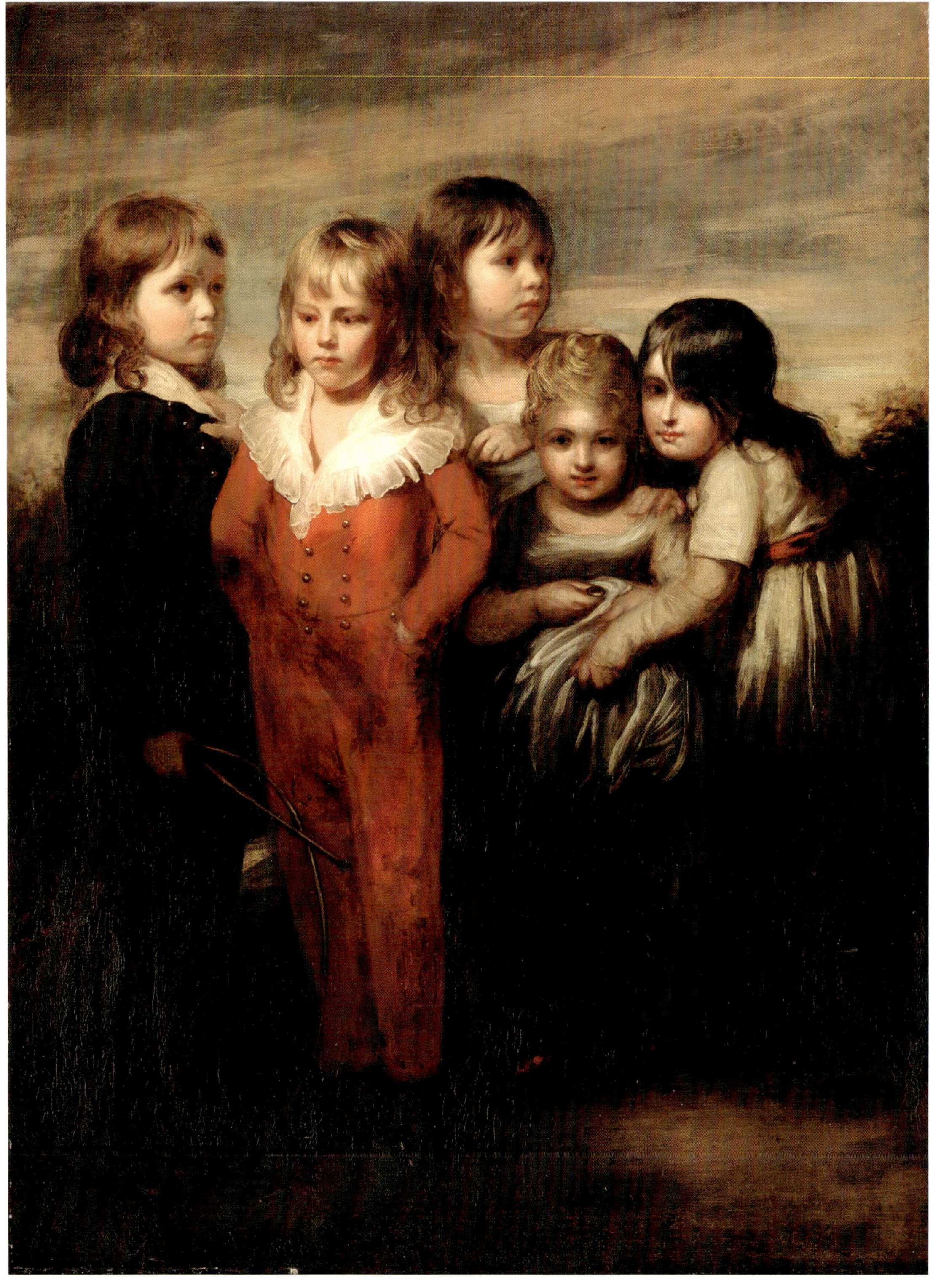

Fig. 43. William Beechey, *The Artist's Children*, c. 1805–10. Oil on canvas, 60 x 45 in. (152.4 x 114.3 cm). Private collection

outside Los Angeles. Huntington had died in 1927. His collection opened to the public in the following year, the most significant art museum in southern California. Kimbell visited in 1939 and the collection bowled him over, becoming his main model in his own collecting efforts. There he would have seen Reynolds's imposing portrait of Sarah Siddons, May Sartoris's great-aunt, in the character of the Tragic Muse. But the work that most charmed and delighted him was Lawrence's *Pinkie* (fig. 21), and this became his touchstone for everything a British portrait should be. Again and again he would urge Newhouse to find him a *Pinkie* of his own. In a letter of 1954, for instance, he reminded him:

> You have been promising me a "Pinkie" for several years. I realize how hard it is to find a picture of that type, but really and truly I do hope that you will find a "Pinkie" in due course of time. As far as I am concerned, that picture of "Pinkie" in California is the most beautiful picture that has ever been painted in the history of the world. If that picture were for sale today, I guess I would have to mortgage my oil wells in order to buy it, and I think I would do that.[85]

By the end of his life Kimbell owned some 360 works of art, including about 200 paintings. Most of the paintings were British, including Reynoldses such as *Anna Ward* (fig. 44), along with Gainsboroughs, Lawrences, and no fewer than 23 portraits by or attributed to George Romney.[86] Although (perhaps in part because) they were childless themselves, he and his wife were always drawn to portraits of children. It was not an uncommon tendency among American Anglophile collectors. If a large part of the appeal of British portraiture was being transported to a better time and place, then the appeal was even more compelling when the sitters were in the Age of Innocence.

On July 5, 1963, now seventy-seven years old, Kay Kimbell wrote to Bertram Newhouse with a familiar refrain: "Find me a Pinkie."[87] Soon afterwards Newhouse offered him Leighton's portrait of May Sartoris, which he bought on October 22. Today most people would consider the work to be first and foremost an example of Victorian painting, and it has become well known as such since appearing on the cover of the catalogue of the landmark exhibition *Victorian High Renaissance*.[88] But Kimbell bought it essentially as a British

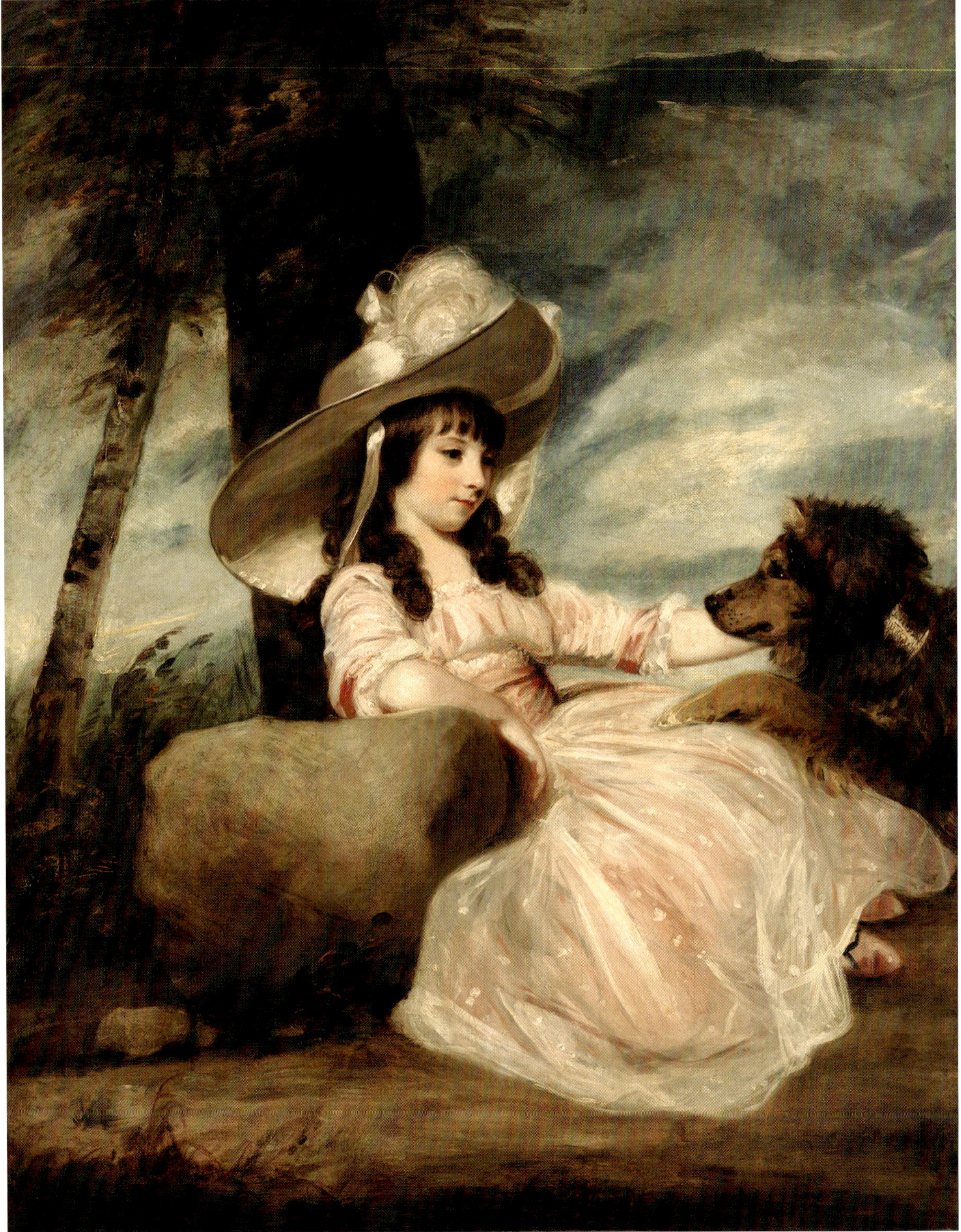

Fig. 44. Joshua Reynolds, *Anna Ward*, 1787. Oil on canvas, 55¾ x 44¾ (141.6 x 113.7 cm). Kimbell Art Museum, Fort Worth

child portrait, presumably without dwelling too much on the fact that it was so much later in date than *Pinkie* and his other favorites of the eighteenth and early nineteenth centuries. When Leighton made the portrait, he was looking at the traditions of British child portraiture much as an outsider, and indeed infused the work with a mood and a view of childhood that were distinctively Victorian. One suspects he would have been nonetheless delighted that his May should have become someone's *Pinkie*. Certainly in quality, interest, and popular appeal, the portrait was the closest Newhouse ever came to satisfying Kay Kimbell's highest and most persistent ambition as a collector. It was not only one of Kimbell's best acquisitions but also one of his last. He died on April 13, 1964, never to see the museum that would bear his name. For a few years after its arrival in Fort Worth the portrait of May hung at Texas Wesleyan College (fig. 45).[89] It took its place in the collection of the Kimbell Art Museum when Louis Kahn's great building opened to the public for the first time in 1972.

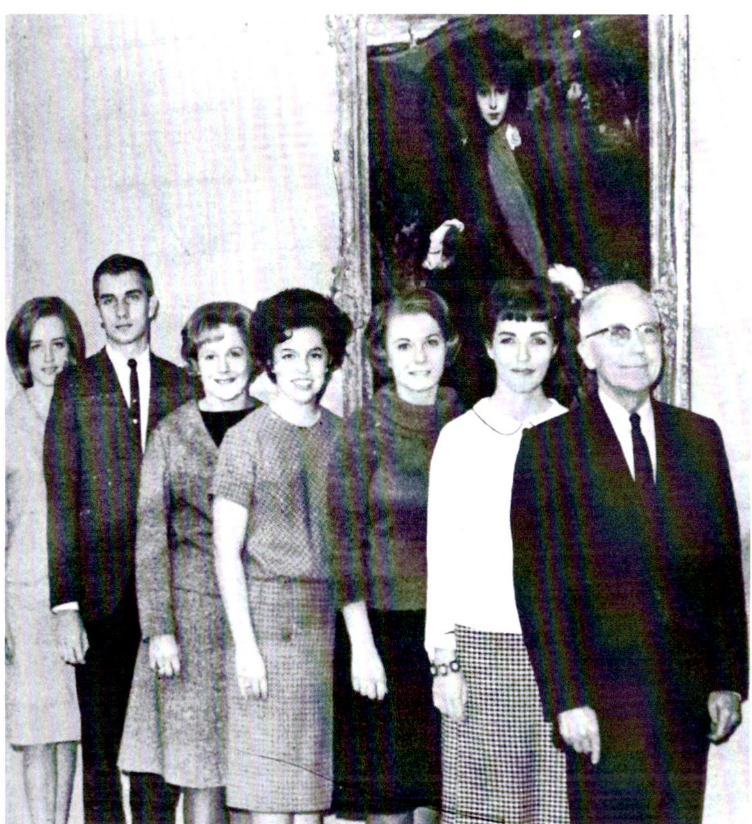

Fig. 45. Officers of the Texas Mu Chapter of Alpha Chi, a national scholarship society, with Dr. Howard Hughes, professor of English, Texas Wesleyan College, Fort Worth, 1966

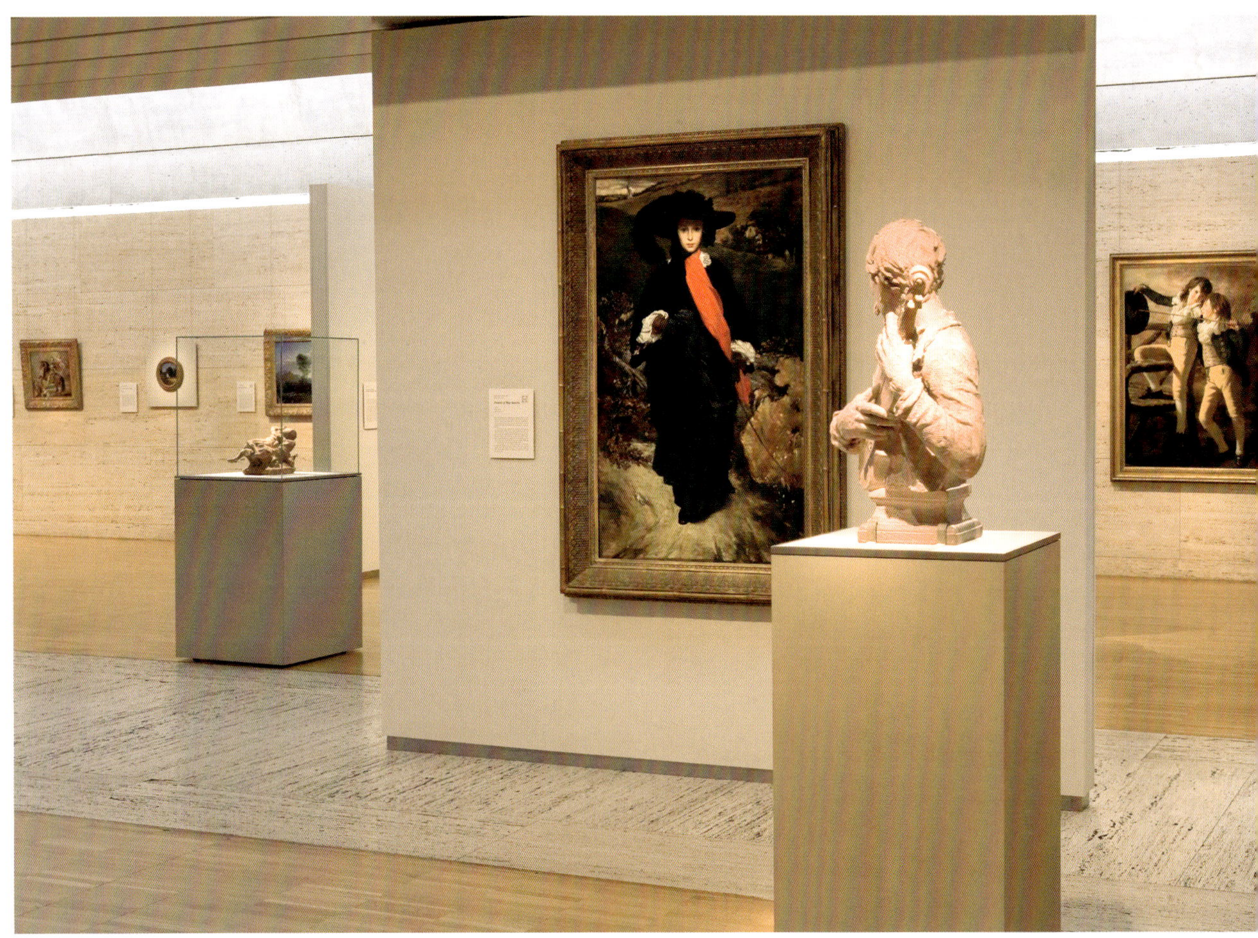

Fig. 46. North galleries, Kimbell Art Museum, Fort Worth, 2009

Acknowledgments

I am much indebted to Ann Blainey for her fine double biography of Fanny and Adelaide Kemble, especially the material from family archives and other collections of Adelaide's letters and papers. My thanks to her, and also to Leonée and Richard Ormond for generously sharing information and discussing ideas about Leighton and his works; Eric Avebury and Lyulph Lubbock for helping me with biographical details about May Sartoris and her descendants; Antoine Sartoris for kindly bringing to my attention works by Leighton still in Sartoris family collections; Deborah Gage, along with Christopher Whittick and Anna Manthorpe at the East Sussex Record Office, for their researches on my behalf into the history of Westbury House; Wilma Picton in Kent, and Michael Blakstad and Paul Andersen in my own native county of Hampshire, for their help with matters of local history and topography; Annette Wickham at the Royal Academy of Arts and Philippa Martin at the Leighton House Museum for guidance with the Leighton drawings in those collections; Cassandra Albinson for help with the Sartoris letters at the Beinecke Library, Yale University; Harold Koda and Stéphane Houy-Towner at the Costume Institute, Metropolitan Museum of Art, and Aileen Ribeiro at the Courtauld Institute of Art for advice on matters of dress; Patricia Cummings Loud at the Kimbell Art Museum for facts and insights about Kay and Velma Kimbell's collecting; Wendy Gottlieb, also at the Kimbell, for editing this book with such care and professionalism; publications assistants Megan Burns and Stefanie Ball Piwetz for gathering the images; and finally Tom Dawson for his outstanding design work on the Kimbell Masterpiece Series.

M. W.

1. Fenn 1903, p. 790.
2. *The Death of Brunelleschi*, 1852; oil on canvas, 101 x 74 in. (256.6 x 186 cm), Leighton House Museum, London. See Ormond 1975, p. 150, pl. 23.
3. *Cimabue's Celebrated Madonna Is Carried in Procession through the Streets of Florence*, 1853–55; oil on canvas, 91¼ x 205⅛ in. (231.7 x 520.9 cm), Royal Collection. See London 1996, pp. 106–7.
4. Jameson 1846, p. 98.
5. Jameson 1846, p. 121.
6. From a letter of July 1848. Thackeray 1945–46, vol. 2, pp. 559–60.
7. Barrington 1906, vol. 1, p. 126.
8. Blainey 2001, p. 187.
9. Jameson 1915, p. 200.
10. From a letter of May 19, 1879. James 1974–84, vol. 2, p. 233.
11. Lord John remained obsessively interested in Adelaide even after her marriage and collected numerous portraits, including the John Hayter pastels to accompany which Anna Jameson wrote "Adelaide Kemble and the Lyrical Drama" (Jameson 1846). Thirty-four of the pastels remain in the Portland Collection at Welbeck Abbey. I am grateful to Derek Adlam, curator of the Portland Collection, for his help with this connection.
12. From a letter to Francis Thun's family, April 7, 1853. Blainey 2001, p. 254.
13. From a letter of August 1848. Chopin 1962, p. 335.
14. For an idea of the leisured, cultured, avidly sightseeing life of the Sartorises in Italy, see Fanny Kemble's memoir *A Year of Consolation* (Kemble 1849), which is dedicated to Edward.
15. Kemble 1891, vol. 1, p. 262. For further details of Adelaide Sartoris's circle in Rome, see Ormond 1975, pp. 20–25.
16. Carr 1908, p. 95.
17. Barrington 1906, vol. 1, p. 166.
18. Barrington 1906, vol. 1, p. 168.
19. Ritchie 1902, pp. ix–x.

20. Sartoris 1865, p. 712.

21. Cowper 1913, p. 54.

22. See Dakers 1996.

23. Barrington 1906, vol. 1, p. 176.

24. Blainey 2001, p. 292.

25. Barrington 1906, vol. 1, p. 128.

26. Sartoris 1867, p. 81.

27. Barrington 1906, vol. 2, p. 57.

28. Barrington 1906, vol. 1, p. 166.

29. Barrington 1906, vol. 1, p. 172.

30. Barrington 1906, vol. 1, p. 183.

31. Joshua Reynolds, *Sarah Siddons as the Tragic Muse*, 1783–84; oil on canvas, 94¼ x 58⅛ in. (239.4 x 147.6 cm), Huntington Library, Art Collections, and Botanical Gardens, San Marino, Calif. See Asleson and Bennett 2001, pp. 368–75. Thomas Gainsborough, *Sarah Siddons*, 1785; oil on canvas, 49¾ x 39¼ in. (126 x 99.5 cm), National Gallery, London. See Egerton 1998, pp. 114–19. For a discussion and anthology of the many portraits of Siddons, see Los Angeles 1999.

32. Fulcher 1856, p. 130.

33. Edward Sartoris left Lawrence drawings of Charles and Fanny Kemble to May in his will (see n. 72, below).

34. Barrington 1906, vol. 1, p.184.

35. On Ingres's portraits of Madame Moitessier, see New York 1999, 426–46. Leighton did meet Ingres during his stay in Paris, writing to his mother: "I have further made the acquaintance of Ingres, who, though sometimes bearish beyond measure, was by a piece of luck exceedingly courteous the day I was presented to him." Barrington 1906, vol. 1, p. 245.

36. Barrington 1906, vol. 2, p. 47.

37. Westbury House was rebuilt after being gutted by a fire in 1904, and the estate was broken up in auction sales in 1918 and 1924. For details of its history, see Collins and Hurst 1967, pp. 56–62; and Standfield 1984, pp. 58–59, 104–6. The house is now a nursing home, and barely a trace of the original landscaping remains.

38. Barrington 1906, vol. 2, p. 52.

39. Barrington 1906, vol. 2, pp. 70–71.

40. Barrington 1906, vol. 2, p. 74.
41. See Ormond 1975, pp. 43–44; and London 1996, pp. 45, 114–16.
42. Sartoris 1880, vol. 2, pp. 83–84.
43. On Leighton's admiration for the Barbizon painters Corot, Millet, Daubigny, and Troyon, see Barrington 1906, vol. 1, p. 241; Ormond 1975, pp. 34–35; and London 1996, pp. 44–45.
44. Stephens 1867, preface.
45. On Lawrence's *Pinkie*, see Asleson and Bennett 2001, pp. 242–48.
46. Blainey 2001, p. 280.
47. Blainey 2001, p. 240.
48. *Helen of Troy*; oil on canvas, 80¾ x 58 in. (205 x 147.5 cm), private collection. Exhibited at the Royal Academy in 1865, this was a landmark in Leighton's development as a painter of classical antiquity. See London 1996, pp. 76–77.
49. In a gossipy letter to Leighton of May 6, 1856, Henry Greville mentioned that Sartoris called on him after seeing the exhibition and that "he likes 'Autumn Leaves.'" Barrington 1906, vol. 1, p. 257.
50. Tennyson 1969, p. 784.
51. For a fuller discussion of the meaning and importance of Millais's painting, see Warner 1984. Millais and Leighton were already beginning to be regarded as the leading British artists of their generation, and also as rivals. Although Leighton disagreed with Pre-Raphaelite ideas, he and Millais admired one another and later became good friends. See Barrington 1906, vol. 1, pp. 187, 234; vol. 2, p. 118; and Ormond 1996.
52. Kemble 1859, pp. 116–17. Fanny takes up the same theme in the following lines from her poem "To ———" (Kemble 1859, p. 146):

    I would my soul might reason then with thine,
    Upon those themes most solemn and most strange,
    Which every falling leaf and fading flower,
    Whisper unto us with a voice divine;
    Filling the brief space of one mortal hour,
    With fearful thoughts of death, decay, and change,
    And the high mystery of that after birth,
    That comes to us, as well as to the earth

53. The Westbury Estate audits are in the Gage/Firle Estate Muniments, East Sussex County Record Office, Lewes (SAS G/HA). In the year ending October 31, 1863, the estate's income from timber was £949 11s. 8½d. and the rent for Westbury House £240. I am grateful to Deborah Gage for kindly searching out this information for me.

54. Leighton designed Barrett Browning's tomb in the Protestant cemetery in Florence. See London 1996, p. 82.

55. The parkland and some buildings survive at Warnford, although the house was demolished in 1958.

56. Blainey 2001, p. 278.

57. Ritchie 1902, p. xxxv.

58. See Ritchie 1902, p. xiii, and Blainey 2001, p. 279.

59. The idea that this figure is a portrait of Edward Sartoris is speculative since there seems, remarkably, to be no verifiable likeness of him extant.

60. Sartoris 1867, pp. 178–79.

61. For a history of Warsash House, which was demolished in 1937, see Woodford 2006, pp. 5–29. The household was recorded as having twelve servants in the 1871 Census (Public Record Office, London).

62. Blainey 2001, p. 295.

63. The only painting by Leighton that May and Henry owned aside from family portraits was *Two Venetian Gentlemen*, about 1862–63; oil on canvas, 38½ x 28½ in. (97.8 x 72.4 cm), private collection. See Ormond 1975, p. 154, pl. 85. This too may have been a wedding gift from the artist.

64. Warsash Lodge survives, now known as Warsash Court. See Woodford 2006, pp. 56–57.

65. Prestons survives, recently renamed Chartres.

66. In the 1891 Census (Public Record Office, London), the family was recorded as residents of 42 Cadogan Gardens, near Sloane Square, with a household of six servants. When Henry made a will on March 18, 1901 (copy provided by Her Majesty's Courts Service, York), he gave his London residence as 59 Cadogan Gardens, with an office at 4 Sun Court, Cornhill.

67. Blainey 2001, p. 307.

68. Sartoris 1880, pp. v–vi.

69. For further information about Algernon Sartoris and his marriage to Nellie Grant, see Gordon 2005.

70. Rosemary was with them at 42 Cadogan Gardens at the time of the 1891 Census, and both she and Vivien were with them at 59 Cadogan Gardens at the time of the 1901 Census (Public Record Office, London).

71. Blainey 2001, p. 302.

72. Edward Sartoris's will is dated July 19, 1887, with a codicil of January 9, 1888 (copy provided by Her Majesty's Courts Service, York). The gross value of his personal estate was resworn in June 1900 at £153,980 17s. 5d.

73. Lubbock 1977, p. 8.

74. Elliot 1925, p. 115.

75. From one of several notebooks in which Leighton wrote down his thoughts on art, Royal Academy of Arts, London, quoted in Ormond 1975, p. 83.

76. Stanzas 5–7 of 9. Swinburne 1904, vol. 6, pp. 376–77.

77. From a letter from a Miss Krout, in Hosmer 1912, p. 345.

78. Lubbock 1977, pp. 29–30.

79. Lubbock 1977, p. 89.

80. On Margaret's acting, see Elliot 1925, pp. 114–15, 264.

81. Adelaide's son Eric Lubbock (May's great-grandson) won the famous Orpington by-election for the Liberal Party in 1962 and served as Liberal Chief Whip in the House of Commons. He succeeded his cousin as Baron Avebury in 1971 and remains active as a Liberal Democrat in the House of Lords.

82. Kimbell Art Museum archives.

83. For a general discussion of the collecting of British art in the United States, see the present author's essay "Anglophilia into Art," in New Haven 2001, pp. 1–18. On Huntington in particular, see Shelley M. Bennett, "The Formation of Henry E. Huntington's Collection of British Paintings," in Asleson and Bennett 2001, pp. 1–15.

84. Beechey painted portraits of six of his children in a "fancy picture" entitled *The Blind Fiddler*. By the early twentieth century this belonged to Beechey's granddaughter Frances Anne Hopkins, also an artist (Roberts 1907, p. 189). It is possible that the present painting is in fact the left side of that work—the right side, which showed the fiddler, a nurse, and the youngest child, having been cut off at some time before its purchase by the Kimbells.

85. Kimbell Art Museum archives.

86. The Kimbells attached no strings to the founding collection, and most has been deaccessioned. The portrait of May and Reynolds's *Anna Ward* are among only eighteen remaining works. Pursuing the aims implied in Kay Kimbell's call for "a museum of the first class" and the mission statement drafted by the first director,

Richard F. Brown, the museum has sought to represent a wide range of world cultures with a small number of works of masterpiece quality (see Patricia Cummings Loud, "The Donor and the Inception of the Museum," and Richard F. Brown, "Policy Statement, June 1, 1966," in Fort Worth 1987, pp. 3–13, 317–18).

87. Kimbell Art Museum archives.

88. See Minneapolis 1978. The portrait was also a star attraction in the Leighton centenary exhibition (see London 1996) and *Great British Paintings from American Collections: Holbein to Hockney* (see New Haven 2001). In the showing of the latter exhibition at the Huntington, it appeared for the first and only time to date in the same galleries as *Pinkie*.

89. For many years the Kimbells had placed works from their collection on long-term loan to Fort Worth institutions, and this continued after Kay Kimbell's death. For information about the portrait of May at Texas Wesleyan College (now University), as well as the photograph from the college yearbook (*TXWECO 1966*, p. 37), I am grateful to Louis K. Sherwood Jr., university archivist.

Bibliography

Asleson and Bennett 2001
Robyn Asleson and Shelley M. Bennett. *British Paintings at the Huntington.* San Marino, Calif., 2001.

Barlow 1999
Paul Barlow. "Transparent Bodies, Opaque Identities: Personification, Narrative and Portraiture." In *Frederic Leighton: Antiquity, Renaissance, Modernity*. Edited by Tim Barringer and Elizabeth Prettejohn. New Haven and London, 1999, pp. 193–219.

Barrington 1906
Mrs. Russell Barrington [Emilie Isabel Barrington]. *The Life, Letters and Work of Frederic Leighton.* 2 vols. London, 1906.

Blainey 2001
Ann Blainey. *Fanny and Adelaide: The Lives of the Remarkable Kemble Sisters.* Chicago, 2001.

Carr 1908
J. Comyns Carr. *Some Eminent Victorians: Personal Recollections in the World of Art and Letters.* London, 1908.

Chopin 1962
Selected Correspondence of Fryderyk Chopin. Translated and edited by Arthur Hedley. London, 1962.

Collins and Hurst 1967
Frances Collins and John Hurst. *Some Chapters of the History of West Meon.* Petersfield, 1967.

Cowper 1913
Countess Cowper [Katrine Cecilia Cowper]. *Earl Cowper, K. G.: A Memoir.* [London?], printed for private circulation, 1913.

Dakers 1996
Caroline Dakers. "Leighton: the truth? Frederic, Lord Leighton, and his relationship with Lily and Fred Mason." *Apollo* 144 (December 1996), pp. 43–47.

Egerton 1998
Judy Egerton. *The British Paintings.* National Gallery Catalogues. London, 1998.

Elliot 1925
W. G. Elliot. *In My Anecdotage.* London, 1925.

Fenn 1903
William Wilthew Fenn. "Recollections of Sir Frederick Leighton." *Chambers's Journal*, 6th ser., 6 (November 14, 1903), pp. 790–93.

Fort Worth 1987
In Pursuit of Quality: The Kimbell Art Museum; An Illustrated History of the Art and Architecture. Edmund P. Pillsbury, Patricia Cummings Loud, William B. Jordan, Emily J. Sano, et al. Fort Worth, 1987.

Fulcher 1856
George Williams Fulcher. *Life of Thomas Gainsborough, R. A.* London, 1856.

Gordon 2005
Christopher Gordon. "A White House Wedding: The Story of Nellie Grant." *Gateway* (Missouri Historical Society) 26 (Summer 2005), pp. 9–19.

Hosmer 1912
Harriet Hosmer. *Letters and Memories*. Edited by Cornelia Carr. New York, 1912.

James 1974–84
Henry James: Letters. Edited by Leon Edel. 4 vols. Cambridge, Mass., 1974–84.

Jameson 1846
Anna Jameson. "Adelaide Kemble and the Lyrical Drama." In *Memoirs and Essays Illustrative of Art, Literature, and Social Morals*. London, 1846, pp. 67–121.

Jameson 1915
Anna Jameson. *Anna Jameson: Letters and Friendships (1812–1860)*. Edited by Mrs. Steuart Erskine. London, 1915.

Kemble 1849
Frances Anne [Fanny] Kemble (Mrs. Butler, late Fanny Kemble). *A Year of Consolation*. 2 vols. New York, 1849.

Kemble 1859
Frances Anne [Fanny] Kemble. *Poems*. Boston, 1859.

Kemble 1891
Frances Anne [Fanny] Kemble. *Further Records, 1848–1883: A Series of Letters*. 2 vols. New York, 1891.

London 1897
Exhibition of Works by the Late Lord Leighton of Stretton, President of the Royal Academy. Exh. cat., Royal Academy of Arts. London, 1897.

London 1996
Frederic Leighton, 1830–1896. Exh. cat. by Stephen Jones, Christopher Newall, Leonée Ormond, Richard Ormond, and Benedict Read. Royal Academy of Arts. London, 1996.

London 2006
A Victorian Master: Drawings by Frederic, Lord Leighton. Exh. cat. by Philippa Martin, Alison Smith, Charlotte Gere, et al. Leighton House Museum. London, 2006.

Los Angeles 1999
A Passion for Performance: Sarah Siddons and Her Portraitists. Robyn Asleson, ed. Exh. cat., J. Paul Getty Museum. Los Angeles, 1999.

Lubbock 1977
Adelaide Lubbock. *People in Glass Houses: Growing up at Government House*. Melbourne, 1977.

Minneapolis 1978
Victorian High Renaissance. Exh. cat. by Richard Dorment, Gregory Hedburg, Leonée Ormond, Richard Ormond, and Allen Staley. Minneapolis Institute of Arts. Minneapolis, 1978.

New Haven 2001
Great British Paintings from American Collections: Holbein to Hockney. Exh. cat. by Malcolm Warner, Robyn Asleson, et al. Yale Center for British Art, New Haven; and Huntington Library, Art Collections, and Botanical Gardens, San Marino, Calif. New Haven, 2001.

New York 1999
Portraits by Ingres: Image of an Epoch. Gary Tinterow and Philip Conisbee, eds. Exh. cat., National Gallery, London; National Gallery of Art, Washington, D.C.; and The Metropolitan Museum of Art. New York, 1999.

Ormond 1975
Leonée and Richard Ormond. *Lord Leighton*. New Haven and London, 1975.

Ormond 1996
Leonée Ormond. "Leighton and Millais." *Apollo* 143 (February 1996), pp. 40–44.

Ritchie 1902
Mrs. Richmond Ritchie [Anne Thackeray Ritchie]. Preface to *A Week in a French Country-House*, by Adelaide Sartoris. London, 1902.

Roberts 1907
William Roberts. *Sir William Beechey, R.A.* London and New York, 1907.

Sartoris 1865
Adelaide Sartoris. "Recollections of the Life of Joseph Heywood, and some of his Thoughts about Music." *Cornhill Magazine* 12 (December 1865), pp. 689–712.

Sartoris 1867
Adelaide Sartoris. *A Week in a French Country-House*. London, 1867.

Sartoris 1868
Adelaide Sartoris. *Medusa, and Other Tales*. London, 1868.

Sartoris 1880
Adelaide Sartoris. *Past Hours*. With a preface by May Evans Gordon. 2 vols. London, 1880.

Standfield 1984
F. G. Standfield. *A History of East Meon*. Chichester, 1984.

Stephens 1867
Frederic George Stephens. *English Children as Painted by Sir Joshua Reynolds*. London, 1867.

Swinburne 1904
The Poems of Algernon Charles Swinburne. 6 vols. London, 1904.

Tennyson 1969
The Poems of Tennyson. Edited by Christopher Ricks. London, 1969.

Thackeray 1945–46
The Letters and Private Papers of William Makepeace Thackeray. 4 vols. Edited by Gordon N. Ray. Cambridge, Mass., 1945–46.

Warner 1984
Malcolm Warner. "John Everett Millais's *Autumn Leaves*: 'A picture full of beauty and without subject.' " In *Pre-Raphaelite Papers*. Edited by Leslie Parris. London, 1984, pp. 126–42.

Warner 1999
Malcolm Warner. "Portraits of Children: The Pathos of Innocence." In *Millais: Portraits*. Exh. cat. by Peter Funnell, Malcolm Warner, et al. National Portrait Gallery, London. Princeton and London, 1999, pp. 105–25.

Woodford 2006
Bryan Woodford. *Warsash and the Hamble River: A History and Guide*. Warsash, 2006.

Photograph Credits

Kimbell Art Museum photography by Robert LaPrelle:
Front cover, frontispiece, figs. 13, 17, 19, 25, 41, 43, 44, 46

© Bolton Museums, Art Gallery, and Aquarium; Bolton Metropolitan Borough Council: fig. 5
By kind permission of His Grace the Duke of Buccleuch and Queensberry, KT: fig. 20
© Christie's Images Ltd.: figs. 22, 33, 38
Prudence Cuming Associates Ltd., London: figs. 3, 4
Courtesy East Sussex Record Office, East Sussex County Council, Lewes: fig. 15
Photographed by Orlando Faria: fig. 6
Courtesy Hampshire County Council Museums and Archives Service: fig. 16
Courtesy The Huntington Library, Art Collections, and Botanical Gardens, San Marino, Calif.: fig. 21
© Keith James, photographer, Hereford: fig. 2
Courtesy Lubbock Family Archives: figs. 28, 39
© Manchester Art Gallery: figs. 24, 37
Photograph © 2007 The Metropolitan Museum of Art, New York: fig. 23
Image © Board of Trustees, National Gallery of Art, Washington, D.C.: fig. 12
Courtesy National Portrait Gallery, London: figs. 1, 27, back cover
Photographed by Wilma Picton: fig. 40
© Edward Reeves, Lewes, East Sussex: fig. 14
Rhea-Engert Photography, Fort Worth: fig. 42
Courtesy Royal Academy of Arts, London: figs. 18, 35
© The Royal Borough of Kensington and Chelsea, Leighton House Museum, London: figs. 10, 29
© The Royal Borough of Kensington and Chelsea, Leighton House Museum, London / The Bridgeman Art Library: fig. 36
© Tate, London, 2007: figs. 8, 9
© V & A Images / Victoria and Albert Museum, London: fig. 26
Courtesy The White House Historical Association, Washington, D.C.: fig. 34